Living Grammar
—New Edition—

by

Atsuko Yamamoto
Naoko Osuka
Chikako Mano
Kyoko Okamoto
Benedict Rowlett

 SEIBIDO

写真提供

ロイター / アフロ（p.113）

アフロ（p.5, 11, 41, 95）

GettyImages / アフロ（p.11, 83）

AFP＝時事（p.59, 65, 107）

dpa / PANA（p.35）

音声ファイルのダウンロード／ストリーミング

CD マーク表示がある箇所は、音声を弊社 HP より無料でダウンロード／ストリーミングすることができます。下記 URL の書籍詳細ページに音声ダウンロードアイコンがございますのでそちらから自習用音声としてご活用ください。

http://seibido.co.jp/ad600

Living Grammar —New Edition—

はしがき

　本書は、ご好評をいただいた2009年度出版『コミュニケーションのためのベーシック・グラマー』の内容を今の時代に沿ったものに作り直したものです。前書と同様、本書は、コミュニケーションに必要な最低限の文法事項を、実際に「使う」ことを経験しながら、わかりやすく楽しく学べることをねらいとしています。

　「英文法を知っていても、実際には英語を使えない」という人は大勢います。本来なら、中学3年間で学ぶ英文法を身につけていれば、かなりのコミュニケーションができるはずなのに、実際には本当に簡単なことすら英語で言えない人が多いのはなぜでしょうか。一つの原因は、文法をコンテクスト（文章の前後の脈絡）から切り離して学んできたことにあると言えるでしょう。知識は大切ですが、単に知識を積み上げるだけでは「使える」ようにはなりません。「使える」ようになるためには、内容中心の言語活動や、実際に意味のあるやり取りをおこないながら文法を学ぶ、という学習方法が有効であると私たちは考えます。また、一方的に知識を与えられるのではなく、学習者自らが文法のルールに気づき理解することも重要です。そのような考えに基づいて作成されたのがこの教科書です。

　本書には以下のような特徴があります。
・学習者が文法知識を確実に理解し使えるようになるために、本書で扱う文法事項は、コミュニケーションに不可欠なものに絞り込んでいます。
・学習者が理解しやすいように、文法事項の説明は簡潔にし、表で示すなど単純明快にしています。
・ユニットごとに内容についてのテーマを設定し、そのテーマについて知識を広げたり考えを深めたりしながら、文法を学べるように構成しています。テーマには、身近な話題や、知的関心が持てるものを選びました。
・各ユニットには、リスニング、リーディング、スピーキング、ライティングの4技能すべてが含まれています。このように文法事項を多角的に使うことによって確実に習得できるようにするとともに、学習者が飽きずに学べるように配慮しました。
・学習者が自ら文法ルールに気づいたり、実際に意味のあるやり取りを経験したりできるように、全体を通して様々なタスク活動を導入しています。

　学習者の皆さんには、文法の知識を得たり理解を深めるだけでなく、実際に「使える」ようになることを是非目指してほしいと思います。本書は、きっとそのお役に立てることと自負しています。また、英語が「使える」ようになるためには、多くの練習が必要なのは言うまでもありません。本書をきっかけとして、英語を「使う」ことの楽しさを実感し、さらなる練習を重ねていただけたら、これほど嬉しいことはありません。

　最後になりましたが、本書の作成にあたっては、成美堂社長佐野英一郎氏と編集部の中澤ひろ子氏に多大なご協力をいただきました。紙面をお借りして厚く御礼申し上げます。

著者

本書の構成と使い方

■ Vocabulary

ユニット内で使用されていて特に重要と思われる10語句が本文に出た順番に並んでいます。ランダムに並んだ日本語と結びつける問題です。

■ Warm-up

ユニットで焦点をあてる文法事項を導入するための、テーマに沿った内容のリスニング問題です。CDを聴いて問題に答えましょう。

■ Grammar Point

ユニットで特に焦点をあてる文法事項を明瞭簡潔に説明しています。

■ Grammar Practice

Grammar Pointで扱った文法事項に関する問題です。2種類の問題形式A, B（各5問）で、BはTOEIC形式の問題です。

■ Dialogue

Grammar Pointで扱った文法事項が会話形式で提示されています。穴埋め問題や入れ替え問題のあとで、対話練習をしてみましょう。

■ Let's check some more!

Grammar Pointや巻末で扱うもの以外で、知っておくと役に立つ文法事項を簡潔に説明しています。

■ Reading

Grammar Pointで扱った文法事項を多く含む、テーマに沿った内容のreadingです。

■ Writing

ユニットで焦点をあてた文法事項を使って、テーマに沿った内容の英文を書く問題です。

CONTENTS

Profile　be動詞

profileとは、人物紹介のことです。このユニットでは、「私は…です」、「彼は…です」といった基本的な文型を使い、人や物の役割や特徴を簡単に説明できるようにしましょう。

■ Vocabulary　英語の意味を下の日本語から選びましょう。　🎧 1-02

1. well-built (　)　　2. slender (　)　　3. talkative (　)　　4. exhausted (　)

5. so-called (　)　　6. currently (　)　　7. outstanding (　)

8. to weigh (　)　　9. innocent (　)　　10. appearance (　)

a. 現在は	b. 傑出した	c. 外見、容姿	d. いわゆる	e. へとへとになった
f. 体格の良い	g. ~の重さがある	h. ほっそりした	i. 無邪気な	j. 話し好きな

■ Warm-up : Ken, His Friend & His Family　🎧 1-03

CDを聞き、4人の人物それぞれの説明としてあてはまるものをボックスの1と2から一つずつ選んで、アルファベットを□に書きましょう。（同じものを何回使っても構いません。）また、ボックスの説明以外に彼らについて聞き取れたことを下線に書きましょう。

1	a. high school student　　b. junior high school student c high school teacher　　d. college student　　e. college teacher f. cram school teacher
2	g. catcher　　h. pitcher　　i. class leader　　j. cheerleader k. mother　　l. grandmother

Ken　□　□

_____

_____

Sho　□　□

_____

_____

Mari　□　□

_____

_____

Yoshiko　□　□

_____

_____

もう一度CDを聞き、下の（　）を埋めて、答えを確認しましょう。 repeat 🔘 1-03

Ken (¹　　　　　) a college student. He is a (²　　　　　) of the college
baseball team. He is a pitcher. He is tall and (³　　　　). Sho is Ken's best
(⁴　　　　　). He is also a college student and a member of the baseball team.
He is a (⁵　　　). He (⁶　　　　　) (⁷　　　　) tall but well-built.
Both Ken and Sho (⁸　　　　) good baseball players. Mari is Ken's sister.
She is a high school student. She is a (⁹　　　). She is pretty and slender.
Yoshiko is their mother. She is an (¹⁰　　　　) teacher at college. She is
friendly and (¹¹　　　). She likes talking with her family and students.

■ Grammar Point : be動詞
「～は …である」＜S＋V＋C＞の文型

▶be動詞は、「～は…である」という文章の「である」に相当します。

肯定文 （補語になるのは 名詞か形容詞）	主語 「～は」	be動詞 「である」	補語 「…」主語の説明をする語
	Ken	is	a college student.（名詞） tall.（形容詞）
	ケンは大学生だ／背が高い。		
否定文 be動詞の後ろに notが入る	主語	be動詞 ＋ not	補語
	Ken	is　　　not （省略形 isn't）	a college student. tall.
	ケンは大学生ではない／背が高くない。		
疑問文 be動詞が 前にくる	be動詞	主語	補語
	Is	Ken	a college student? tall?
	ケンは大学生ですか／背が高いですか？		

▶be動詞は、「（～に）いる／ある」という存在の意味を表すこともあります。

Ken is in the classroom.	ケンは教室にいる。
Our school is in Yokohama.	私たちの学校は横浜にある。

▶主語によるbe動詞の使い分けに注意しましょう。

代名詞が主語のとき					
主語（単数）	be動詞	省略形	主語（複数）	be動詞	省略形
I	am	I'm	we	are	we're
you	are	you're	you	are	you're
he	is	he's	they	are	they're
she	is	she's			
it	is	it's			

名詞が主語のとき	
主語	be動詞
単数	is
複数	are

Grammar Practice

A. （　）内の語を並べ替えて、意味の通る英文にしましょう。

1. (player, brother, my, is, a, tennis).

　　_____

2. (Aya, classmates, and, are, I).

　　_____

3. (the, are, intelligent, very, sisters).

　　_____

4. (grammar, not, is, difficult, English).

　　_____

5. (parents, teachers, your, are, college)?

　　_____

B. 選択肢の中で最も適切なものを選び、1〜5の英文を完成させましょう。

1. Both Ayumi and Nancy _____ twenty years old.
   (A) is   (B) am   (C) are   (D) was

2. The chairs in the meeting room _____ comfortable. They're too old.
   (A) is   (B) isn't   (C) are   (D) aren't

3. _____ Mr. Brown an English teacher or a French teacher?
   (A) Am   (B) Are   (C) Does   (D) Is

4. I have three brothers. One of them _____ a police officer.
   (A) am   (B) is   (C) are   (D) have

5. All the members of my club _____ exhausted now after training hard.
   (A) is   (B) are   (C) was   (D) were

■ Dialogue   🎧 1-04

対話文を聞いた後、ペアで ☐ の部分を入れ替えて練習しましょう。最後は、☐ の部分を自分で考えて対話練習しましょう。

Nina introduces herself to Ken at a ballpark.

Nina: Hi. I'm Nina. I'm an exchange student from ⌐Canada⌐.¹ Nice to meet you.

Ken: Nice to meet you, too, Nina. I have a friend in ⌐Toronto⌐.² Are you from ⌐Toronto⌐?²

Nina: No, I'm not. I'm from ⌐Vancouver⌐.³ It's a large city in western ⌐Canada⌐.¹

	1. 国名	2. 都市名	3. 都市名
対話 ①	Australia	Sydney	Perth
対話 ②	Germany	Berlin	Frankfurt
対話 ③	Switzerland	Zurich	Geneva

Let's check some more!

● be動詞の現在形は am, is, are の３つです。主語に応じて使い分けます。
● 特に主語の数（単数か複数か）には注意が必要です。
   （例）**One** of the most popular baseball players **is** Shohei Ohtani.
   　　　　　　　　　　　　（最も人気のある野球選手の一人は…です。）

Reading : *Shohei Ohtani* 1-05

Shohei Ohtani is one of the most popular Japanese baseball players today. He was born on July 5, 1994, in Oshu, Iwate as the youngest of three children. He was a so-called "yakyu shonen" – a kid who lives and breathes baseball. After playing in the Nippon Professional Baseball Organization (NPB), he moved to play Major League Baseball (MLB) in America. Currently, he is a member of the Los Angeles Angels. Shohei is an outstanding two-way player. He is good at both batting and pitching, so he is often called the Babe Ruth of our time. His powerful physique supports his special talent. He is very tall and well-built. Actually, he is 6 feet 4 inches tall and weighs about 210 pounds. In spite of his size, he is shy and charming. He is still like an innocent "yakyu shonen." His talent, appearance, and personality are all the secrets of his popularity.

live and breathe ~ ～に熱中する **physique** 体格 **foot**（単位）約30cm（feetは複数形）
inch（単位）約2.5cm **pound**（単位）約0.45kg

A. 彼のProfileを英語で表にまとめましょう。

Profile Table	
Name	
Date of birth / Place of birth	
Occupation	
Team	
Talent	
Appearance	
Personality	
Others	

B. 次の文が英文の内容と合っていればT、合っていなければFと書きましょう。

1. Shohei Ohtani is from Iwate Prefecture. (　　)
2. He belongs to an NPB team. (　　)
3. He is not only a good batter but also a good pitcher. (　　)
4. He likes "yakyu shonen." (　　)
5. He is very popular because he is innocent. (　　)

Writing

A. 以下はある学生の自己紹介のスピーチの原稿です。 これを読んで、この学生のprofileを
   表（Table 1）にまとめましょう。 1-06

> Hello, everyone. My name is Miki Nakano. I am 19 years old and a freshman at college. My major is economics. I don't study very hard. I am busy with other activities. I belong to the dance club. I am not a good dancer, but I love dancing. I am also a member of the chorus club. I like singing with other people. I have several close friends. They say I am friendly and funny. I think they are funny, too. I have a part-time job. I am a cashier in a convenience store. I am happy when people smile at me. I want to enjoy my college life. Thank you for listening.

Profile Table 1	
Name	
Age	
Occupation	
Major	
Club	
Part-time job	
Personality	
Others	

Profile Table 2	
Name	
Age	
Occupation	
Major	
Club	
Part-time job	
Personality	
Others	

B. 次に、Profile Table 1を参考にして、自分のprofileを上の表（Table 2）に記入して
   みましょう。そして、この表をもとにして、自分の自己紹介文を書いてみましょう。

_____

_____

_____

_____

_____

_____

_____

_____

Sports 一般動詞 (1)

このユニットでは、現代の私たちの生活に欠かせないスポーツを題材に、「私は−します」、「彼は…を−します」といった英語の基本的な表現を学びましょう。

■ Vocabulary 英語の意味を下の日本語から選びましょう。 🎧 1-07

1. to bet ( )   2. to last ( )   3. to pass ( )   4. protective ( )
5. to discuss ( )   6. to raise ( )   7. to lie down ( )
8. for example ( ) 9. to chase ( )   10. to participate ( )

a. 参加する	b. 追う	c. 続く	d. 横になる	e. 例えば
f. (手などを) 上げる	g. 賭ける	h. 保護用の	i. 話し合う	j. 渡す

■ Warm-up : What Do You Know about Sports?

A. それぞれのスポーツに関連する語を下のボックスから選び、アルファベットを下線に書きましょう。該当するものをすべて選びましょう。

a. egg-shaped ball	b. sword	c. bet	d. gym	e. 90 minutes	f. helmet

B. CDを聞いて、どのスポーツについて述べられているのか、番号を□に書きましょう。

🎧 1-08

A. _____ □   B. _____ □   C. _____ □

D. _____ □   E. _____ □   F. _____ □

もう一度CDを聞き、下の ( ) を埋めて、答えを確認しましょう。　repeat　CD 1-08

1. In fencing, two people (　　　　　　　) with swords.
2. Many people (　　　　　　) money on horse racing.
3. A game of soccer (　　　　　　) for 90 minutes.
4. In rugby, you (　　　　　　) an egg-shaped ball by hand.
5. Some people (　　　　　) to a gym to take aerobics classes.
6. In American football, players (　　　　　　) a helmet and protective clothing.

■ Grammar Point：一般動詞 (1) 自動詞・他動詞

　　　　　　　　　「～は／ーする」　　　＜S＋V＞の文型
　　　　　　　　　「～は／…を／ーする」＜S＋V＋O＞の文型

▶動詞 { be動詞 (am, is, areなど)
　　　　一般動詞 { 自動詞 (目的語をとらない)
　　　　　　　　　他動詞 (目的語をとる)

▶一般動詞はbe動詞以外の動詞で、人や事物の状態や動作を表します。

肯定文 主語が3人称単数の時は、動詞に -s (-es)をつける	主語 「～は」	動詞 「ーする」		目的語* 「…を」	(修飾語句)
	I	go (自)		(なし)	to a gym.
	私はジムに行く。				
	A player	passes (他)		a ball.	
	選手はボールを渡す。				
否定文 do/does notの後は動詞の原形	主語	do not (don't) does not (doesn't)	動詞 (原形)	目的語 「…を」	(修飾語句)
	I	do not (don't)	go	(なし)	to a gym.
	私はジムに行かない。				
	A player	does not (doesn't)	pass	a ball.	
	選手はボールを渡さない。				
疑問文 Do/Doesが文頭 主語の後の動詞は原形	Do/Does	主語	動詞 (原形)	目的語 「…を」	(修飾語句)
	Do	you	go	(なし)	to a gym?
	あなたはジムに行きますか。				
	Does	a player	pass	a ball?	
	選手はボールを渡しますか。				

8

＊目的語とは「～は…を－する」という文の「…を」にあたり、主語の動作が及ぶ対象になる語です。名詞・代名詞か名詞に代わる語が目的語になります。

【注意すべき点】

①こんな間違いに注意しましょう。

I ~~am~~ go to school. ~~Are~~ Do you go to school?

②日本語からの類推で自動詞か他動詞か混同しやすい単語があります。

自動詞 …… agree (with, to), complain (about/of) など

他動詞 …… approach, attend, discuss, enter, leave, marry, reach, resemble など

③自動詞か他動詞かで意味が異なる動詞があります。自動詞run「走る」、他動詞run「経営する」など

④まぎらわしい自動詞と他動詞があります。自動詞lie「横になる」、他動詞lay「横にする」など

■ Grammar Practice

A. （　）の中の語を並べ替えて、意味の通る英文にしましょう。ただし、一つだけ余分な語があります。

1. (play, I, and, practice, Tom, judo) every weekend.

   _____

2. (aerobics, Mary, does, play, not, do).

   _____

3. (Judy, on, is, watch, does, sports) television?

   _____

4. Mary (discuss, I, about, rules, the, and) of the game after school.

   _____

5. Please (right, your, hand, rise, when, raise) you feel pain.

   _____

B. 選択肢の中で最も適切なものを選び、1～5の英文を完成させましょう。

1. Julie wants to _____ a baseball player like Ichiro.

   (A) marry with　　(B) marry　　　　(C) get married　　(D) marry to

2. My sister _____ the famous golf player Hinako Shibuno.

   (A) look like　　(B) looks like　　(C) looks　　　　(D) looks alike

3. Many Japanese people _____ sumo tournaments on TV.

    (A) look   (B) see   (C) watch   (D) view

4. Don't _____ down here even if you are tired.

    (A) lay   (B) lain   (C) laid   (D) lie

5. You have to _____ at the station at seven sharp to join the tennis training camp.

    (A) arrive   (B) reach   (C) come   (D) get

▮ Dialogue

CDを聞いて、対話文の（　　）を埋めましょう。ペアで対話練習をしましょう。　　🅒 1-09

Akira and Julie are talking about sports.

Akira: (　　　　　　) you (　　　　　　) any sports?

Julie: Yes, I (　　　　　) snooker.

Akira: I (　　　　) (　　　　　　) snooker. Do you (　　　　)?

Julie: No, you don't.

Akira: Well, (　　　　) you (　　　　　) a ball or something?

Julie: You (　　　　　) a cue or a stick.

Akira: I (　　　　　). Is it like billiards?

Julie: Yes, that's right.

Let's check some more!

● 動詞のあとに前置詞があれば、自動詞です。例えば、同じ意味の文章でも、"He goes to school." の 'go' は自動詞ですが、"He attends school." の 'attend' は、他動詞になります。

● 多くの動詞は自動詞としても他動詞としても使われます。

  （例）The door opened suddenly.　He opened the door suddenly.

Reading : *Crazy Sports of the World* 🎧 1-10

Bog snorkelling

Cheese chasing

Everybody knows soccer, golf, and tennis, but do you ①<u>know</u> that there are hundreds of crazy sports around the world? For example, in England, you can ②<u>try</u> "bog snorkelling" and "cheese chasing." People go bog snorkelling in central England. You ③<u>need</u> a mask, a snorkel, and flippers. You ④<u>swim</u> in a race in muddy water. In the west of England, people ⑤<u>chase</u> a big cheese down a hill. Hundreds of people ⑥<u>participate.</u> In South Australia, there is a tuna-throwing sport. You ⑦<u>need</u> a big fish, and you ⑧<u>throw</u> it as far as you can. Many strong people also ⑨<u>participate</u> in Finland's wife carrying sport. You ⑩<u>carry</u> your wife in a race. The champion ⑪<u>wins</u> a lot of beer! Which crazy sport do you ⑫<u>want</u> to try?

....

flippers ひれ足　**muddy** 泥の　**tuna** マグロ

A. 下線部の一般動詞は、自動詞なのか他動詞なのかを考えましょう。

B. 下の表の空欄を英語で埋めてみましょう。

	どこで？	必要なものは？	やり方は？
Bog snorkelling	in central England		
Cheese chasing			
Tuna-throwing			
Wife carrying			

Writing

A. 以下のeメールを読みましょう。一般動詞に下線を引いて、自動詞なのか他動詞なのか考えてみましょう。 🎧 1-11

Hi,

My name is Carol. I live with my family in New York. My husband works for a bank. He plays golf on weekends. I have one son and one daughter. My son goes to high school. He practices gymnastics. My daughter does not live with us. She studies economics at college. She belongs to a swimming club and swims very fast. I am a busy homemaker, but in my free time I do aerobics. My family are all athletic and like sports a lot. What sports do you like? Do you have any sports specific to Japan? Please write to me and let me know about yourself and about some popular sports in Japan. I am looking forward to your reply.

Best,

Carol

practice gymnastics 器械体操をする

do aerobics エアロビクス体操（有酸素運動）をする

B. アメリカ人のCarolに返事を書きましょう。簡単な自己紹介の後に、①自分の好きなスポーツとその説明、好きな理由、②日本で人気のあるスポーツとその説明、人気のある理由などについて、できるだけ詳しく、Carolが興味を持つように書きましょう。

Hi Carol,

_____

_____

_____

_____

_____

_____

_____

_____

_____

_____

Unit 3

Special Occasions 一般動詞 (2)

人生の特別な日に、人は贈り物をあげたり特別な言葉をかけたりします。このユニットでは、「(人)に〜をあげる」、「(人)を〜にする」など、Unit 2よりも少し難しい表現ができるように学習しましょう。

■ Vocabulary 英語の意味を下の日本語から選びましょう。 🅲 1-12

1. occasion (　　)　　2. in exchange (　　)　　3. to name (　　)
4. Dutch (　　)　　5. to provide (　　)　　6. to register (　　)
7. certificate (　　)　　8. registration (　　)　　9. without a doubt (　　)
10. unforgettable (　　)

| a. 登録 | b. (特別な) 時 | c. 間違いなく | d. (〜と) 引き換えに | e. オランダの |
| f. 命名する | g. 提供する | h. 忘れられない | i. 登録する | j. 証明書 |

■ Warm-up : Birthday Gifts for Miho

以下は、小学生のミホが書いた作文「私の誕生日」に登場する人たちです。それぞれの人物の説明を読み、誰がミホにどんな贈り物をしたのかを下のボックスから推測して選び、アルファベットを□に書きましょう。

<u>Grandparents</u>—live in the countryside. Miho doesn't meet them so often.
<u>Aunt</u>—enjoys cooking.
<u>Kumi</u>—is Miho's best friend. She knows that Miho likes brand-name goods.
<u>Eri</u>—likes to take pictures with her friends.
<u>Uncle</u>—lives in the U.S. He is talkative.
<u>Parents</u>—always buy special gifts for their children on special occasions.

| a. bag | b. cake | c. dress | d. telephone call | e. puppy | f. photo frame |

Grandparents　□　　Aunt　□　　Kumi　□

Eri　□　　Uncle　□　　Parents　□

🐶 CDを聞いて、答えをチェックしましょう。 🅲 1-13

もう一度CDを聞き、下の（　）を埋めて、答えを確認しましょう。　repeat　○CD 1-13

I like my birthday. It is the most exciting day of the year. Every year many people (¹   ) me a lot of presents. My grandparents (²   ) me a dress. I wear it on my birthday. My aunt (³   ) a delicious birthday cake for me. I eat it with my friends at my birthday party. They (⁴   ) me various gifts. For example, Kumi gave me a brand-name bag this year. Eri gave me a photo frame with our picture in it. My uncle in America usually (⁵   ) me a call at night. He (⁶   ) me interesting stories about his life in a foreign country. My parents always (⁷   ) me a big present. This year they gave me a puppy. I named her Happy. Now she is my best friend. She really (⁸   ) me happy.

■ Grammar Point：一般動詞 (2) 二重目的語、目的語と補語をとる動詞
「〜は／…に／…を／ーする」　　＜S＋V＋O₁＋O₂＞の文型
「〜は／…を／…に（と）／ーする」＜S＋V＋O＋C＞の文型

▶一般動詞の中には、目的語を一つではなく二つ（二重目的語）とるものがあります。

＜S＋V＋O₁＋O₂＞の文型 O₁＝「(人)に」, O₂＝「(物)を」 この文型では、授与動詞と呼ばれる動詞が使われ、「give型」と「buy型」に分けられる*¹	主語 「〜は」	動詞 「ーする」	間接目的語 「(人)に」	直接目的語 「(物)を」
	Kumi	gives	me	a bag.
	クミが私にバッグをくれる。			
	My aunt	bakes	me	a cake.
	叔母が私にケーキを焼いてくれる。			

＜S＋V＋O＋to / for...＞の文型への転換 目的語の「(物)を」を先に置く場合には、(人)の前に前置詞のtoかforが必要になる*²	主語 「〜は」	動詞 「ーする」	目的語 「(物)を」	前置詞 to/for	… （人）
	Kumi	gives	a bag	to	me.
	クミが私にバッグをくれる。				
	My aunt	bakes	a cake	for	me.
	叔母が私にケーキを焼いてくれる。				

*¹ give型：give, lend, send, show, teach, tellなど
　 buy型：buy, bake, cook, find, get, makeなど

*² give型の動詞は前置詞のtoをとり、buy型の動詞はforをとる。

▶動詞の後に目的語＋補語が続く場合は、目的語＝補語の意味です。この場合の補語は目的語を説明しています。補語になるのは名詞か形容詞です。

＜S＋V＋O＋C＞の文型 よく使われる動詞は、believe, call, find, get, keep, leave, make, name, thinkなど	主語 「〜は」	動詞 「－する」	目的語 「…を」	補語 「…に（と）」
	I	named	the puppy	Happy.
	私は子犬を「ハッピー」と名付けた。(the puppy =Happy)			
	She	makes	me	happy.
	彼女は私を幸せにする。(me = happy)			

Grammar Practice

A. （　）内の語句を並べ替えて、意味の通る英文にしましょう。

1. (happy, the present, me, makes, very).

   _____

2. My friend often (in, his, me, dictionary, lends, English class).

   _____

3. (we, new, the, student, Jim, call).

   _____

4. I (her, birthday, my mother, some flowers, send, on).

   _____

5. (you, do, send, Christmas cards, your friends, to) in America ?

   _____

B. 選択肢の中で最も適切なものを選び、1〜5の英文を完成させましょう。

1. You never _____ us the truth.
   (A) talk   (B) say   (C) speak   (D) tell

2. I _____ the question very difficult.
   (A) know   (B) find   (C) have   (D) ask

3. Keep in touch. Please write a letter _____ me.
   (A) to   (B) for   (C) at   (D) on

4. Your son has a cold, so you need to keep the room _____.
   (A) cool   (B) warm   (C) clean   (D) busy

5. I don't like this color. Could you _____ me another?
   (A) sell   (B) teach   (C) look   (D) show

▌Dialogue

対話文を聞いた後、ペアで ☐ の部分を入れ替えて練習しましょう。最後は、☐ の部分を自分で考えて対話練習しましょう。 🎧 1-14

Erika asks Andy for a favor.

Erika: Could you help me with some ☐English☐?[1] I want to write a letter to my pen pal in ☐the U.S.☐[2]

Andy: OK. Will you teach me some ☐Japanese☐[3] in exchange? I find it difficult.

Erika: No problem. Please ask me anything you want.

	1. 言語	2. 国名	3. 学習内容
対話 ①	French	France	kanji
対話 ②	Chinese	China	English
対話 ③	Spanish	Spain	German

Let's check some more!

● He gives me a gift. と He makes me happy. とは、文型が違うことに注意しましょう。最初の文章は me（間接目的語）≠ a gift（直接目的語）ですが、後の文章は me（目的語）＝happy（補語）（つまり I am happy）である点がポイントです。

Reading : *A Romantic Gift* 🔘 1-15

If you want to give your girlfriend or boyfriend a romantic gift on a special occasion, here is a good idea. How about buying him or her a star? You can name a star after your loved one. If you pay more, you can even buy two close stars or binary stars at once. Then you can name the other one after yourself. A Dutch company provides people around the world this gift service. Just visit their website, and you can register. They will send you a certificate of registration and a star map. Show the certificate to your special person and look up in the night sky. Without a doubt, you can make the next special occasion an unforgettable one.

binary star 連星

A. 下線部の動詞には二つの目的語があります。間接目的語（…に）は○で囲み、直接目的語（…を）は□で囲みましょう。

B. 次の文が英文の内容と合っていればT、合っていなければFと書きましょう。

1. If you pay money, you can own a star.   (   )

2. You can buy only one star at one time.   (   )

3. A company in the Netherlands provides this service.   (   )

4. People in any country can buy and name a star.   (   )

5. This gift is not suitable for Christmas.   (   )

■ Writing

A. 以下のeメールを読みましょう。二つの目的語が続く動詞に下線、目的語＋補語が続く動詞に二重線を引きましょう。 (CD) 1-16

> Hi Mari,
>
> How are you? Thanks for your e-mail. Today I'll tell you about my favorite holiday, Easter. Easter is one of the most popular holidays in America. It's in spring. Many people attend church to celebrate the resurrection of Jesus Christ. We also decorate eggs in bright colors. We call them Easter eggs. We hide them, and children hunt them. Children believe a rabbit, the Easter Bunny, brings them the eggs. They also eat Easter eggs made of chocolate. Easter makes children really happy!
>
> What kind of festivals do you have in Japan? Please tell me something about Japanese festivals.
>
> Thanks,
>
> Carol

resurrection キリストの復活

B. アメリカ人のCarolに返事を書きましょう。日本の年中行事や祭りを一つ紹介しましょう。

（例）正月 New Year's Day　　　　　成人の日 Coming-of-Age Day
　　　節分 Bean-Throwing Ceremony　ひな祭り Girls' Festival / Doll Festival
　　　花見 Cherry-blossom Viewing
　　　端午の節句（こどもの日）Boys' Festival (Children's Day)
　　　七夕 Star Festival　　　　　　盆 Bon Festival
　　　七五三 Shichigosan (Seven-Five-Three) Festival

_____

_____

_____

_____

_____

_____

_____

_____

Unit 4

Families 人称代名詞

人称代名詞は、話し手や相手をさしたり、すでに話題に上った人、物、事について述べるときに使います。このユニットでは、さまざまな家族を話題にして、人称代名詞の使い方を学びましょう。

■ Vocabulary　英語の意味を下の日本語から選びましょう。　(CD) 1-17

1. chief (　)　　　　2. tribe (　)　　　　3. beard (　)　　　　4. desert (　)

5. office worker (　)　　6. mathematics (　)　　7. to keep up with (　)

8. meal (　)　　　　　9. popular with (　)　　10. successful (　)

a. 食事	b. 種族	c. 成功した	d. 〜に遅れない	e. 数学	f. あごひげ
g. 砂漠	h. 長、かしら	i. (事務職の) 会社員	j. 〜に人気の		

■ Warm-up : World Families

1〜5の人々はどの少数民族に属すると思いますか？ボックスから選んで名前の下にアルファベットを書きましょう。

a. Ainu (Hokkaido)	b. Aborigine(Australia)	c. Inuit (Canada)
d. Native American (USA)	e. Maori (New Zealand)	

1. Wakcha
_____

2. Ariki

3. Yukie
_____

4. Lutaaq
_____

5. David
_____

 CDを聞いて、答えをチェックしましょう。　 1-18

もう一度CDを聞き、下の(　)を埋めて答えを確認しましょう。　repeat　CD 1-18

1. Hi, I'm Wakcha, a native American from the USA. I live with my father.
   (　　　) is the chief of our tribe. Everybody likes (　　　).
2. My name's Ariki. I'm a Maori from New Zealand. (　　　) often have
   tattoos on our bodies.
3. I'm Yukie. I am a member of an Ainu family from Hokkaido. (　　　)
   husband has a very long beard!
4. Hello. My name's Lutaaq. I live in the north of Canada with my family. We
   are Inuit. It is very cold, so we wear (　　　) (　　　) (　　　) fur.
5. G'day. I'm David. My parents are Aboriginal Australians. (　　　) live in
   the desert, but I live in the city.

▮ Grammar Point : 人称代名詞

▶代名詞は、名詞の繰り返しを避けるために、その代わりに用いられる語です。
▶人称代名詞は人称・格・数によって変化します。

	単数			複数		
	主格 〜は、〜が	目的格 〜を、〜に	所有格 〜の	主格 〜は、〜が	目的格 〜を、〜に	所有格 〜の
一人称	I	me	my	we	us	our
二人称	you	you	your	you	you	your
三人称	he	him	his	they	them	their
	she	her	her			
	it	it	its			

主格 … 文の主語の働きをします。

I have a brother. He likes motorbikes. (私には弟がいる。弟はバイクが好きだ。)

My parents are very active. They like travelling.

(両親は活動的だ。両親は旅をするのが好きだ。)

目的格 … 動詞や前置詞の目的語として用いられます。

I am lost. Please help me. (道に迷いました。私を助けてください。)

It is my brother's birthday next week. I will give him a present.

(来週は兄の誕生日だ。兄にプレゼントを贈るつもりだ。)

所有格 … 所有格の次には名詞がきます。

My sister is a nurse.（私の妹は看護師です。）

Please tell me your telephone number.（あなたの電話番号は何ですか？）

［注意すべき点］

前述の名詞について言及する場合、その名詞が単数扱いになるのか複数扱いになるのか注意する必要があります。

I have two brothers. — They are office workers.

Where are my scissors? — They are on your desk.

Do we need money to live a happy life? — Yes, it is important.

■ Grammar Practice

A. 英語ではすでに話題にのぼった名詞を代名詞で置き換えます。上の英文の ☐ の部分を適当な代名詞に変えて下の英文を完成させましょう。

例：**My sister is a teacher.** My sister **teaches mathematics.**

　→**My sister is a teacher. She teaches mathematics.**

1. My parents live in Tokyo. My parents love Tokyo.

　→My parents live in Tokyo. _____ love Tokyo.

2. The city is very big. The city is very old, too.

　→The city is very big. _____ is very old, too.

3. My mother's name is Sarah. My mother's hobby is dancing.

　→My mother's name is Sarah. _____ hobby is dancing.

4. It is my girlfriend's birthday tomorrow. I will give my girlfriend a present.

　→It is my girlfriend's birthday tomorrow. I will give _____ a present.

5. I live in Hokkaido with my family. I love my family very much.

　→I live in Hokkaido with my family. I love _____ very much.

B. 選択肢の中で最も適切なものを選び、1〜5の英文を完成させましょう。

1. My friend gives _____ a CD for my birthday every year.

   (A) my   (B) me   (C) him   (D) he

2. Can you see my glasses? _____ are usually on my desk.

   (A) Their   (B) It   (C) They   (D) Them

3. I go to Hokkaido every summer. _____ is a wonderful place.

   (A) There   (B) Here   (C) She   (D) It

4. Is John at home? I want to ask _____ a question.

   (A) him   (B) her   (C) his   (D) he

5. I want to say thank you to your parents. Do you have _____ telephone number?

   (A) their   (B) our   (C) my   (D) them

■ Dialogue

対話文を聞いた後、ペアで ☐ の部分を入れ替えて練習しましょう。最後は、☐ の部分を自分で考えて対話練習しましょう。 (CD) 1-19

Tomomi is asking John about his family.

Tomomi: Do you have a big family?

John:　　 Not really. I have one brother and one sister .¹

Tomomi: Please tell me more.

John:　　 My brother is an office worker, and my sister is a scientist .²

	1. 兄弟姉妹	2.（兄弟姉妹の）説明
対話 ①	a younger sister	She's a high school student
対話 ②	two older brothers	They're in college
対話 ③	a twin brother	We look exactly the same, but we have very different personalities

Let's check some more!

● 主格we, you, theyは特定の人々ではなく、一般の人々をさす場合があります。

　(例) They speak English in Australia.

● 人称代名詞を2つ以上並べる場合、2人称→3人称→1人称の順序が一般的です。

　(例) My brother and I visit our grandparents once a month.

22

Reading : *The Kardashians* 1-20

The Kardashians are a very famous American family. The main members of the Kardashian family are Kris Jenner and ①<u>her</u> daughters, Kourtney, Kim, Khloe, Kendall, and Kylie. ②<u>They</u> have a reality TV show, "Keeping Up with the Kardashians." ③<u>It</u> is about ④<u>their</u> everyday lives in California. ⑤<u>They</u> go shopping, have family meals, and meet ⑥<u>their</u> friends. ⑦<u>It</u> is very popular with people all around the world. People like ⑧<u>them</u> because ⑨<u>they</u> are glamorous and successful. For example, Kim and Kylie have make-up and fashion businesses, and Kendall is a model.

....

The Kardashians カーダシアン一家　**reality TV show** リアリティテレビ番組
glamorous 魅惑的な　**make-up and fashion businesses** 化粧品とアパレル会社

A. 下線部の代名詞が、誰または何を指しているか考えましょう。

B. 例文を参考にして、下の文を完成させましょう。

Example: The Kardashians are British.
　　　　　　No, they are American.

1. The Kardashian family has three members.

　　No, _____

2. Their TV show is about their friends.

　　No, _____

3. The TV show is only popular in America.

　　No, _____

4. People dislike the Kardashians.

　　No, _____

5. Kendall is a fashion designer.

　　No, _____

Writing

A. 以下の英文を読みましょう。 1-21

My father's name is Bill. He was born in California and raised in New York, but now he lives in Hawaii. He is married to my mother, and they are very happy. My father is a police officer, and he is very busy. In his free time, he likes surfing and playing music. He plays the ukelele in a band. He often plays it for tourists.

B. 自分の家族や親戚の一人についての情報を下の表に書きましょう。

Relation 自分との関係	
Married/Single 既婚 / 未婚	
Home 住まい	
Job 仕事	
Hobby 趣味	
Other information 他の情報	

C. 表をもとにして自分の家族や親戚の一人について書きましょう。

_____

_____

_____

_____

_____

_____

_____

_____

Japan Quiz Wh-疑問文

あなたは日本についてどれくらい知っているでしょうか？このユニットでは、日本についてのさまざまなクイズに挑戦しながら、Wh-Questions、つまり What や Where などで始まる疑問文について学びましょう。

■ Vocabulary 英語の意味を下の日本語から選びましょう。 (CD) 1-22

1. to consist of (　)　　2. population (　)　　3. emperor (　)　　4. temple (　)
5. similar (　)　　　6. capital (　)　　　7. imperial (　)　　　8. current (　)
9. prime minister (　)　　10. to bow (　)

| a. 寺 | b. おじぎをする | c. 類似した | d. 天皇 | e. 首相 |
| f. 首都 | g. 人口 | h. 〜から成る | i. 現在の | j. 皇室の |

■ Warm-up : How Much Do You Know about Japan?

クイズを読んで正解と思うものに○をしましょう。

1. How many prefectures does Japan consist of?
   a) 28　　　　b) 35　　　　c) 47　　　　d) 55

2. What is the population of Japan?
   a) 70 million　b) 100 million　c) 130 million　d) 180 million

3. Who is the emperor of Japan at present?
   a) Hirohito　b) Naruhito　c) Haruhito　d) Akihito

4. Where is Sensoji Temple?
   a) in Tokyo　b) in Kyoto　c) in Nara　d) in Osaka

5. Why are there so many sumo wrestlers from Mongolia?

   Because they _____ .

   a) have a similar culture　　b) have a similar sport
   c) like Japan　　　　　d) learn Japanese at school

 CDを聞いて、答えをチェックしましょう。 1-23

Japan is an island country in East Asia. It consists of (^{1}) prefectures including Tokyo, Hokkaido, Osaka, and Kyoto. About (^{2}) (^{3}) people live in Japan. Japan has an emperor. He is the symbol of the country. At present (^{4}) is the emperor. The Japanese people love cherry blossoms very much. They bloom in spring. In Tokyo there are many (^{5}) blossom viewing spots. For example, walking along the Sumida River near Sensoji (^{6}), you can find many cherry trees. The Japanese (^{7}) sport is sumo. These days, many sumo wrestlers are from foreign countries. There is a type of wrestling very (^{8}) to sumo in Mongolia. That's why we see so many Mongolian sumo wrestlers.

▌ Grammar Point : Wh-疑問文

▶Yes か No かではなく、具体的な情報を尋ねるために疑問詞で始まる疑問文を使います。
▶疑問詞の種類と疑問文の語順は以下の通りです。

Who 誰？	Who＋疑問文〜？
	Who is that girl? － She is Judy, my daughter. Who(m) do you meet every weekend? － I meet my friends.
	Who＋動詞〜？ (who が主語の場合)
	Who comes here every day? － My best friend does.
What 何？	What＋疑問文〜？
	What is your favorite sport? － My favorite sport is tennis. What do you do every weekend? － I play mahjong.
	What＋動詞〜？ (what が主語の場合)
	What makes you happy? － Good food and wine.
When いつ？	When＋疑問文〜？
	When is your birthday? － My birthday is February 14. When do you study? － I study at night.
Where どこで？	Where＋疑問文〜？
	Where is Sensoji Temple? － It's in Asakusa. Where do you live? － I live in Kyoto.

Why なぜ？	Why+疑問文〜？
	Why is it red? － Because it represents the rising sun. Why do you study English? － To make foreign friends.
How どのように？	How+疑問文〜？
	How are your family? － They are fine, thanks. How do you go to school? － By bus.

■ Grammar Practice

A. 次の（　）内の語句を並べ替えて、意味の通る英文にしましょう。

1. (what, you, want, eat, do, to) for dinner?

_____

2. (do, study, why, English, you)?

_____

3. (is, English teacher, who, your)?

_____

4. (does, Mr. Gibson, live, where)?

_____

5. (many, are, there, how, English classes) in a week?

_____

B. 選択肢の中で最も適切なものを選び、1〜5の英文を完成させましょう。

1. A : _____ does your school year begin?

   B : In April.

   (A) What   (B) When   (C) Where   (D) How long

2. A : _____ is the capital of Japan?

   B : Tokyo.

   (A) When   (B) Where   (C) How   (D) What

3. A : _____ lives in the Imperial Palace?

    B : The Imperial family does.

    (A) Where   (B) What   (C) Who   (D) When

4. A : _____ do most people in Tokyo get to work?

    B : By bus and train.

    (A) How   (B) Where   (C) What   (D) When

5. A : _____ is Tokyo Tower?

    B : 333 m.

    (A) How much   (B) How tall   (C) How old   (D) How far

▮ Dialogue

（　　）に適当な疑問詞を入れて対話文を完成させましょう。その後でCDを聞いて答えを確認し、最後にペアで対話練習をしましょう。 🎧 1-24

Hillary and Taku are talking on campus.

Hillary: (　　　　　　　) do you live, Taku?

Taku: In Asakusa.

Hillary: (　　　　　　　) is Asakusa famous for?

Taku: Asakusa is famous for Sensoji Temple.

Hillary: (　　　　　　　) long does it take you to come to school?

Taku: Two hours. (　　　　　　) about you?

Hillary: It takes me only five minutes. I live near the campus.

Let's check some more!

- whatの後には名詞、howの後には形容詞、副詞などがつくことがあります。
  - （例）what color, what sport, what subject, what time
    - how big, how long, how many （〜）, how much （〜）, how old, how fast, how often
- Why? は口語でHow come? で代用されることがあります。How comeに続く語順は主語＋動詞？になるので注意しましょう。
  - （例）Why are you late? = How come you are late?

Reading : *Common Questions about Japan* 1-25

These days Japanese culture, such as Japanese food, language, and animation, is getting popular around the world. Now many people outside Japan enjoy sushi and buy T-shirts with kanji on them. People in many foreign countries watch Japanese animation on TV. There is, however, still a lack of understanding about Japan and Japanese people. Here are some common questions asked by foreign people : Do Japanese people eat sushi every day? Where is Japan? Who is the current Prime Minister of Japan? How do Japanese children learn kanji? Why do Japanese people bow? If Japanese people expect foreign people to understand Japan, they should be ready to answer such questions. To do that, Japanese people need to understand more about themselves first. How many of the questions above can you answer?

expect 人 to 〜 人が〜することを期待する

A. Wh-疑問文に下線を引きましょう。そのうち3つの質問に英語で答えましょう。

_____

_____

_____

_____

_____

B. 次の文が英文の内容と合っていればT、合っていなければFと書きましょう。

1. These days Japanese music is especially popular with young people around the world. ( )

2. Nowadays many foreigners know every detail about Japanese culture. ( )

3. Japanese people need to know more about their own country. ( )

Writing

A. 以下はある学生の午前中の過ごし方です。下線部を尋ねる疑問文を下の表（Table 1）に書き入れましょう。 🎧 1-26

> This is a typical weekday morning for me. I get up at ①7 every morning. I jog and take a shower ②before breakfast. I eat two pieces of toast, an egg, and a salad. I also drink ③a cup of coffee. I leave home for school ④at 8 o'clock. I walk to the station. ⑤At a convenience store near the station, I buy a box lunch. I meet ⑥a friend of mine there, and we go to school ⑦by train.

B. 次に、表（Table 1）を参考にして、パートナーに聞きたい質問を表（Table 2）に書き出しましょう。

Table 1	Table 2
① What time do you get up?	
② When _____ ?	
③	
④	
⑤	
⑥	
⑦	

C. 質問の答えをもとにしてパートナーの平日の過ごし方について下に書きましょう。

_____

_____

_____

_____

_____

_____

_____

_____

Love and Marriage 過去形

恋愛と結婚はいつの時代でも人々の関心事です。このユニットでは、歴史上の人物や現代の有名人の恋愛と結婚を話題にしながら、「～だった」という過去のできごとを話す表現を学びましょう。

■ Vocabulary 英語の意味を下の日本語から選びましょう。 🎧 1-27

1. century (　　)
2. ancient (　　)
3. to get married (　　)
4. to get engaged (　　)
5. to fall in love (　　)
6. to break up (　　)
7. fairy tale (　　)
8. long-distance relationship (　　)
9. establish (　　)
10. ideal (　　)

a. おとぎ話	b. 理想的な	c. 恋に落ちる	d. 別れる	e. 古代の
f. 長距離恋愛	g. 設立する	h. 世紀	i. 婚約する	j. 結婚する

■ Warm-up : Famous Couples

下の5つの出来事の起こった時期を推測してボックスから選び、アルファベットを□に書きましょう。（1つ余分な選択肢があります。）

a. in the 16th century	b. in 2011	c. in ancient times
d. in 2020	e. in 1993	f. in the mid 60's

1. Caesar and Cleopatra fell in love □

2. Prince William and Catherine Middleton got married □

3. Masako Owada and Crown Prince Naruhito got engaged □

4. John Lennon and Yoko Ono got to know each other □

5. Shakespeare and Ann Hathaway got married □

 CDを聞いて、答えをチェックしましょう。 🎧 1-28

31

もう一度ＣＤを聞き、下の（　）を埋めて、答えを確認しましょう。　**repeat**　1-28

Here are some love affairs and marriages of famous people in the past and in modern times. In ancient times, Caesar (^{1}) in love with Cleopatra when he (^{2}) 52 years old. Cleopatra was about 20 years old. William Shakespeare and Ann Hathaway (^{3}) (^{4}) in the 16th century. Shakespeare was 18 and Ann was 26. John Lennon (^{5}) to know Yoko Ono in London in 1966, and they got married in 1969. Emperor Naruhito first (^{6}) Empress Masako in the 80's. At that time, Naruhito was the Crown Prince of Japan, and Masako was a student at the University of Tokyo. They got engaged in January and (^{7}) their wedding ceremony in June, 1993. Crown Prince William and Catherine Middleton (^{8}) dating in 2003 when they (^{9}) students at the University of St Andrews. They once (^{10}) up, but finally got engaged in 2010 and married in April, 2011.

■ Grammar Point：過去形

▶過去形は、過去にあった状態や動作・できごとなどを表すのに使います。

be動詞 (was / were)　　　　　　　　　一般動詞

肯定文
Mary was famous five years ago. メアリーは5年前有名だった。
否定文　be動詞の後ろにnotが入る
Mary was not famous five years ago. メアリーは5年前は有名でなかった。
疑問文　Be動詞が前にくる
Was Mary famous five years ago? メアリーは5年前有名でしたか？

肯定文
Mary got engaged in 2003. メアリーは2003年に婚約した。
否定文　動詞の前にdid notが入る
Mary did not get engaged in 2003. メアリーは2003年には婚約しなかった。
疑問文　Didが前に入り、動詞が原型になる
Did Mary get engaged in 2003? メアリーは2003年に婚約しましたか？

▶be動詞の過去形は主語によって以下のように変化します。

主語（単数）	be動詞	主語（複数）	be動詞
I	was	we	were
you	were	you	were
he	was		
she	was	they	were
it	was		

▶一般動詞の過去形には規則動詞と不規則動詞があります。

規則動詞：動詞の原形＋ed　　　　　　不規則動詞

現在形	過去形
live	lived
play	played
stop	stopped
study	studied

現在形	過去形
break	broke
bring	brought
cut	cut
get	got

※語尾が短母音＋子音の場合は子音字を重ねます。（例）stop→stopped
※語尾が子音字＋yの場合はyをiに変えてedをつけます。（例）study→studied

■ Grammar Practice

A. 間違いを訂正して、全文を書き直しましょう。

1. My mother is a nurse 10 years ago.

   ＿＿＿＿＿＿＿＿＿＿＿＿＿＿＿＿＿＿＿＿＿＿＿＿＿＿＿＿

2. Did you busy the day before yesterday?

   ＿＿＿＿＿＿＿＿＿＿＿＿＿＿＿＿＿＿＿＿＿＿＿＿＿＿＿＿

3. My sister and her boyfriend break up last month.

   ＿＿＿＿＿＿＿＿＿＿＿＿＿＿＿＿＿＿＿＿＿＿＿＿＿＿＿＿

4. I do not like mathematics when I was in high school.

   ＿＿＿＿＿＿＿＿＿＿＿＿＿＿＿＿＿＿＿＿＿＿＿＿＿＿＿＿

5. Sho and Ken do not play baseball last weekend.

   ＿＿＿＿＿＿＿＿＿＿＿＿＿＿＿＿＿＿＿＿＿＿＿＿＿＿＿＿

B. 選択肢の中で最も適切なものを選び、1～5の英文を完成させましょう。

1. ＿＿＿＿ your father play golf last Sunday?
   (A)Was　　　　　(B) Were　　　　　(C) Do　　　　　(D) Did

2. My mother _____ me a new jacket last Christmas.
   (A) buys   (B) buy   (C) bought   (D) bring

3. A: Were you in the library yesterday afternoon?
   B: Yes, I _____.
   (A) did   (B) am   (C) were   (D) was

4. _____ they go shopping last Saturday?
   (A) Do   (B) Are   (C) Were   (D) Did

5. When did your son _____ engaged to her?
   (A) get   (B) gets   (C) got   (D) is

■ Dialogue

対話文を聞いた後、ペアで ☐ の部分を入れ替えて練習しましょう。最後は、 ☐ の部分を自分で考えて対話練習しましょう。 (CD) 1-29

Karen and Pat are talking about their first loves.

Karen: When did you fall in love for the first time?

Pat: At the age of ☐7☐ .¹ I fell in love with ☐one of my classmates☐ .²

Karen: Why did you fall in love?

Pat: Because she was ☐cute and kind☐ .³

	1. 年齢	2. 誰	3. 理由
対話 ①	5	Sailor Moon	strong and cool
対話 ②	8	my brother's friend	friendly and smart
対話 ③	12	my piano teacher	tall and beautiful

Let's check some more!

● 過去形の疑問文と否定文では主語に関係なく did が使われます。動詞が原形になることに注意しましょう。
   （例）Did he go shopping yesterday? No, he didn't. He didn't go shopping.
● 過去を表す語句には次のようなものがあります。
   ~ago（~前） at that time（その当時） the day before yesterday（おととい）
   last~（この前の~） the week before last（先々週）

Reading : *A Modern Fairy Tale* 1-30

Mary, a young Australian woman, met Frederik, a handsome European man, at a bar in Sydney during the 2000 Summer Olympics. When they met, Mary did not know anything about him. Frederik was actually the Crown Prince of Denmark. They fell in love with each other and started dating.  After Frederik went back to Denmark, they kept a long-distance relationship. Frederik sometimes visited Australia secretly to see Mary. In 2002, Mary moved to Denmark, and they got engaged in 2003. Crown Prince Frederik and Mary got married in May, 2004, and now they have four children. In 2007, she established the Mary Foundation to solve many serious social problems in the world and received an international award for her work in 2014.

the Mary Foundation メアリー財団

A. 二人の出会いから結婚までのできごとを表にまとめましょう。

Time	Events
In 2000	
After the Olympics	
In 2003	
In 2004	
In 2007	
In 2014	

B. 1〜5の質問文を読んで英語で答えましょう。

1. Did Mary know who Frederik was when she met him for the first time?

_____

2. Was Frederik the King of Denmark when he met Mary?

_____

3. Did Mary and Frederik keep up their relationship after he went back to Denmark?

_____

4. Did Mary move to Denmark right after the Sydney Olympics?

   _____

5. Do you want to marry a prince/princess?

   _____

▋ Writing

A. 以下はある学生の書いた作文です。これを読んで、書いてある内容を表（Table 1）にまとめましょう。 🎵 1-31

> When I was a junior high school student, I saw an old movie with my father in the living room after dinner. The title of the movie was *Roman Holiday*. A young, slender girl with black hair, Audrey Hepburn, was in the movie. The movie was beautiful, and Audrey was so charming. When I saw her brilliant eyes and friendly smile, I fell in love with her. After that, I watched many of her movies such as *Breakfast at Tiffany's* and *My Fair Lady*. When I knew she was no longer alive, I was very sad. These days I do not watch her movies anymore, but I still like her very much. She is my ideal woman.

B. 次に、表（Table 1）を参考にして、自分が誰かを好きになった体験について表（Table 2）に記入してみましょう。スターでも身近な人でもかまいません。

Table 1		Table 2	
Name その人の名は	Audrey Hepburn	Name	
Time 好きになった 時期は	when he was a high school student	Time	
Reason どうして		Reason	
Place どこで		Place	
Beginning きっかけは	He watched her movie with his father.	Beginning	
After that その後は	He watched many of her movies.	After that	
Now 今は		Now	

C. 表（Table 2）をもとにして短い英文を書いてみましょう。

Unit 7

Life History 現在完了形 (1) 継続

英語での自己紹介や就職の面接などでは、過去の活動と今も継続して行っている活動を区別して表現する必要があります。このユニットでは、その表現の違いを理解し自分で使い分けができるようにしましょう。

■ Vocabulary 英語の意味を下の日本語から選びましょう。 🎧 1-32

1. to graduate (　　)
2. to enter (　　)
3. to purchase (　　)
4. economics (　　)
5. company (　　)
6. no wonder (　　)
7. activist (　　)
8. climate (　　)
9. to inspire (　　)
10. politician (　　)

a. 政治家	b. 感化する	c. 会社	d. 購入する	e. 卒業する	f. 入学する
g. 経済学	h. どうりで	i. 活動家	j. 気候		

■ Warm-up : Takuya's Life History

A. それぞれの絵に合うできごとを下のボックスから選んでアルファベットを下線部に書きましょう。

a. was born　　b. graduated from high school
c. played rugby in a school team　　d. entered college　　e. started working

🎧 B. 次にCDを聞いて、起きたできごとの順に□に番号を入れましょう。 🎧 1-33

1. □
2. □
3. □

4. □
5. □

37

もう一度CDを聞き、下の（　）を埋めて、答えを確認しましょう。　repeat　CD 1-33

Takuya (¹　　　　) (²　　　　　　) in Niigata in 1994. He (³　　　　　　)
from high school in 2013. He (⁴　　　　　　) college in Tokyo in 2014. In his
first year, he (⁵　　　　　) a member of the rugby team. He (⁶　　　　　　)
from college and (⁷　　　　　) working for a bank in 2018. He (⁸　　　　　)
(⁹　　　　　　) for the bank for more than three years. He (¹⁰　　　　　　)
(¹¹　　　　　) a member of the bank rugby team since 2018.

Takuyaのlife historyをtime lineに表すと次のようになります。

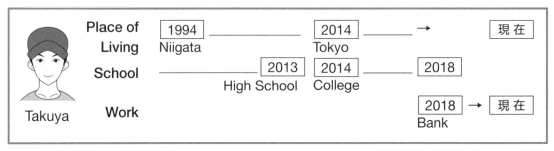

注：→はその状態が継続していることを意味します。

◤ **Grammar Point**：現在完了形(1) 継続
　　　　　　　　　＜have / has＋過去分詞＞で「(過去から)〜している」を表す

▶現在完了形と過去形の違い

現在完了形 have/has+ 過去分詞	過去のできごとが現在までつながっている場合に使う		
	He has worked for a bank	since 2018.	2018年から
		for 10 years.	10年間
		since he graduated from college.	大学を卒業して以来
	彼は銀行でずっと働いている。(今も働いている)		
過去形 動詞+ed (または 不規則形)	できごとが過去に終わっている場合に使う		
	He worked for a bank	10 years ago.	10年前に
		for 10 years.	10年間
		in 2018.	2018年に
		when he was young.	若い頃に
	彼は銀行で働いていた。(もう働いていない)		

＊He / She has や I have は、He / She's や I've と省略することができます。

肯定文	have (has)＋過去分詞	He has worked for a bank since 2018.
否定文	have (has) not＋過去分詞	He has not worked for a bank since 2018.
疑問文	Have (Has)＋主語＋過去分詞〜?	Has he worked for a bank since 2018?

▓ Grammar Practice

A. （　）内の適語を選んで○をしましょう。

Rui Hachimura is a professional basketball player. He (was born/has been born) in Toyama Prefecture in 1998. He (started/has started) playing basketball when he was in junior high school. He (graduated/has graduated) from Meisei High School in Sendai in 2016. He (lived/has lived) in the United States since he entered Gonzaga University in 2016. In 2019, he (became/has become) an NBA (National Basketball Association) player.

B. 選択肢の中で最も適切なものを選び、1〜5の英文を完成させましょう。

1. A: When _____ you purchase your house in Tokyo?
   B: Ten years ago.
   (A) did   (B) have   (C) are   (D) were

2. Taro _____ his job in 2006, but since then, he has studied economics.
   (A) has lost   (B) lost   (C) lose   (D) loses

3. Ted's girlfriend baked a cake for Ted. He _____ sick since he ate it.
   (A) have been   (B) was   (C) has been   (D) being

4. Five years have passed since I _____ working for the company.
   (A) started   (B) have started   (C) start   (D) am

5. A: How long have you been married?
   B: I have been married _____.
   (A) Ten years ago   (B) in 2005   (C) when I was 25   (D) for 50 years

▮ Dialogue

CDを聞いて対話文の（　）を埋めましょう。ペアで対話練習をしましょう。　🎧 1-34

Lilian and Michael are talking about Michael's life in Japan.

Lillian:　How long (　　　　) (　　　　) (　　　　) in Japan?

Michael:　I've been here (　　　　) 12 years.

Lillian:　12 years!　When (　　　　) you come here?

Michael:　(　　　　) I was 6.

Lillian:　No wonder you speak Japanese so well.

Reading : *Greta Thunberg* 1-35

Greta Thunberg is a young Swedish climate activist. She was born in 2003 and (① began/ has begun) her activism when she was only 15. She (② protested / has protested) outside the Swedish Parliament for three weeks in August 2018 to call for action to stop climate change. Since then, inspired by Greta, many other school children around the world (③ held / have held) their own climate change protests. Lately, Greta (④ received / has received) many prizes for her activism. In 2019, three Norwegian politicians (⑤ nominated / have nominated) her for the Nobel Peace Prize. In the same year, she (⑥ appeared / has appeared) on the cover of *Time* magazine and is now famous throughout the world. Although Greta has Asperger's syndrome, this (⑦ did not stop/ has not stopped) her from communicating her important message – if we don't stop climate change, our planet will not have a future.

....

Swedish Parliament スウェーデン国会議事堂　**Nobel Peace Prize** ノーベル平和賞
Asperger's syndrome アスペルガー症候群

A. （　　）内の適語を選んで○をしましょう。

B. 質問文を読んで英語で答えましょう。

1. When was Greta born?

　　_____

2. When did she start her activism?

　　_____

3. What have other school children done since then?

　　_____

4. When was she nominated for the Noble Peace Prize?

　　_____

5. What is Greta's message to the world?

　　_____

▌Writing

A. あなた自身のlife historyをtime lineで表しましょう。□には年号を入れましょう。

```
Place of Living    [      ] (        ) [      ] (        ) [      ] (        ) →

School             [      ] (        ) High School [      ] (        ) College →

Hobby/Club         [      ] (        )              [      ] (        ) →
```

B. 次の質問に答えましょう。

1. When and where were you born?

   _____

2. Where do you live now?

   _____

3. When did you graduate from high school and enter college?

   _____

4. What do you study at college?

   _____

5. Did you belong to any club at high school and do you belong to any club at college?

   _____

C. 上の表と質問の答えを参考にして自分のlife historyを書きましょう。過去形と現在完了形の両方を使いましょう。

   _____

   _____

   _____

   _____

   _____

Leisure 現在完了形 (2) 経験・完了

映画・音楽鑑賞や、スポーツ、旅行などの余暇活動は、日常会話で最もよく話題になります。
「〜をもう聞いた?」、「〜したことある?」、「〜をまだ見たことがない」といった表現を学び
ましょう。

■ Vocabulary 英語の意味を下の日本語から選びましょう。 (CD) 1-36

1. challenging (　)　 2. to play a role (　)　 3. amusement park (　)
4. worth ~ (　)　　　 5. experience (　)　　 6. resort (　)
7. personally (　)　　 8. countless (　)　　　 9. ride (　)　　 10. staff (　)

a. 〜するに値する　　b. 経験　　c. 個人的には　　d. 〜の役を演じる　　e. 数えきれないほどの	
f. 職員、スタッフ　　g. 行楽地　　h. (遊園地などにある) 乗物　　i. やりがいのある　　j. 遊園地	

■ Warm-up : Have you ever ~?　Have you ~ yet?

イラストを見ながら二人の会話を聞きましょう。質問に対する答え (Yes か Never/No か、
回数) にチェックを入れましょう。 (CD) 1-37

1.

☐ Yes
(☐1 ☐2 ☐3〜)
☐ Never

2.

☐ Yes
(☐1 ☐2 ☐3〜)
☐ Never

3.

☐ Yes
(☐1 ☐2 ☐3〜)
☐ Never

4.

☐ Yes
☐ No

5.

☐ Yes
☐ No

6.

☐ Yes
☐ No

もう一度CDを聞き、（　）を埋めて、質問と答え方の両方を確認しましょう。

repeat 🎧 1-37

1. A: Have you ever (　　　　　　) to Tokyo Tower?
   B: Yes. I've (　　　　) there (　　　　).
2. A: Have you ever (　　　　) mahjong?
   B: Yes. I've (　　　　) it (　　　　) (　　　　).
3. A: Have you ever (　　　　) sushi?
   B: No. I've (　　　　) (　　　　) any Japanese food.
4. A: Have you (　　　　　) the Academy Award-winning movie yet?
   B: Yes. I've (　　　　) (　　　　) it.
5. A: Have you (　　　　　) today's newspaper (　　　　)?
   B: No. I haven't (　　　　) it (　　　　).
6. A: Have you (　　　　) lunch yet?
   B: Yes. I've (　　　　) (　　　　) it.

▆ Grammar Point : 現在完了形 (2) 経験・完了

<have/has＋過去分詞>で「～したことがある」、
「～したところだ、～してしまった」を表す

▶現在完了形には、継続用法 (Unit 7) のほかに、経験用法と完了（結果）用法があります。

継続	（ずっと）～だ	He has worked for a bank since 1996. 彼は1996年からずっと銀行で働いている。
	for（～間）、since（～以来）などの期間を示す副詞句を伴うことが多い。	
経験	～したことがある	She has been to Tokyo Tower twice. 彼女は東京タワーに2回行ったことがある。
	never（決して～ない）、ever（かつて）、once（一度）、twice（二度）、 ～times（～回）、before（以前に）などの副詞（句）を伴うことが多い。	
完了 （結果）	～したところだ ～してしまった （→だから今…だ）	He has just gone out. 彼はちょうど出かけたところだ。
		I have already read today's newspaper. 私はもう今日の新聞を読んでしまった。
		She has not finished her homework yet. 彼女はまだ宿題を終えていない。
	just（ちょうど）、already（すでに）、yet（いまだ～ない）などの副詞を伴うことが多い。通常alreadyは肯定文、yetは疑問文と否定文で使う。	

Grammar Practice

A. (　　) 内の語を並べ替えて、意味の通る英文にしましょう。

1. (already, the, we, movie, seen, have).

   _____

2. (he, never, eaten, food, has, Thai).

   _____

3. (have, phone call, received, just, a, I).

   _____

4. (not, they, finished, yet, work, have, the).

   _____

5. (you, ever, gone, have, fishing)?

   _____

B. 選択肢の中で最も適切なものを選び、1～5の英文を完成させましょう。

1. Keiko has lived in New York for 5 years. She _____ the musicals on Broadway several times.
   (A) has seen　　　(B) was seeing　　　(C) sees　　　(D) see

2. They _____ back from vacation only yesterday.
   (A) come　　　(B) came　　　(C) has come　　　(D) have come

3. When _____ to a karaoke bar?
   (A) you last went　　　　　　(B) did you last go
   (C) have you last gone　　　　(D) do you last go

4. The actress says the drama is challenging. She _____ played a role like this before.
   (A) has　　　(B) has ever　　　(C) has never　　　(D) wasn't

5. I cannot get into the theater. I _____ my ticket.
   (A) lose　　　(B) have been lost　　(C) have lost　　　(D) am losing

■ Dialogue

文末の日本語を参考にして対話文の（　　）に適語を入れましょう。その後で、CDを聞いて答えを確認し、ペアで対話練習をしましょう。 ((°CD)) 1-38

Gary calls Junko and asks her out.

Gary: Hi, Junko. (　　　　　) you (　　　　　) your homework yet?

[（もう）終わった]

Junko: Yes, I (　　　　　) just (　　　　　) it. Now I'm free. [終わったところだ]

Gary: David and I are planning to go to the Yomiuri Land Amusement Park this afternoon. Would you like to come with us?

Junko: I'd love to. (　　　　　) never (　　　　　) to Yomiuri Land.

(　　　　　) you ever (　　　　　) there? [～に行ったことがある]

Gary: Yes, (　　　　　). [2回] It's great fun. Can we meet at Yomiuri Land Station at noon?

Junko: No problem. See you then.

Let's check some more!

● 「～に行ったことがある」という経験を表すには have been to～ が一般的です。
have gone to～ は「行ってしまった（もうここにいない）」の意味になります。
● already, just は通常 have と過去分詞の間に置かれます。(already を文末に置くと意味が強調されます。)
(例) He has already read the book. (彼はもうその本を読んだ。)
(例) He has read the book already. (彼はもうその本を読んだのですか！)
● yet は通常文末に置かれます。
(例) He hasn't read the book yet. (彼はまだその本を読んでいない。)

Reading : *Weblog*

ウェブ掲示板でのメールのやりとりを読みましょう。 (CD) 1-39

Have you ever been to Disneyland or Disney World in the US? I haven't. Is it worth visiting? Tell me about your experiences at the resorts. (Kate)

***** ***** ***** ***** ***** ***** ***** *****

Yes, I have been to both, once each. Personally I love Disney World in Florida much more. It's for the whole family. People of all ages can enjoy the magic world. (Amy)

I have lived near Disneyland in California for most of my life, so I have been there countless times since it opened in 1955. It's really fun, but there are always long lines for popular rides. (Tom)

I have been to Disney World several times since its opening in 1971. All the rides are very exciting and the staff there are wonderful. (Liz)

I have been to Disneyland. And, actually, I have just come back from my first visit to Disneyland Paris. It opened in 1992, the year of my birth. I really enjoyed it. I could get on most rides without waiting so long. (Mark)

A. 文中の現在完了の部分に下線を引きましょう。

B. 質問文を読んで英語で答えましょう。

1. Where are Disneyland and Disney World?

_____

2. Which resort has the longest history?

_____

3. Who has probably visited a Disney resort the most?

_____

4. Who has visited Disney World?

_____

5. What is the biggest difference between Disneyland in California and Disneyland Paris?

_____

Writing

A. 以下の英文を読みましょう。 📀 1-40

When I was a child, I often went skiing with my family. Recently, however, I have started to enjoy snowboarding. I have gone snowboarding five times. I have been to Nagano and Yamagata. I enjoy snowboarding because it is very fast and exciting. I also think that it looks cool. Next year I want to go to Hokkaido because I have never gone snowboarding there. People say the snow in Hokkaido is very good.

B. 娯楽や、スポーツ、観劇、旅行などを題材に自由に書いてみましょう。できるだけ現在完了形を使いましょう。

_____

_____

_____

_____

_____

_____

_____

_____

_____

_____

_____

_____

_____

_____

_____

_____

_____

_____

_____

_____

Unit 9

College Life 進行形

様々な活動で忙しい大学生生活。このユニットでは、そんな学生生活を題材に、習慣的活動を言うときの「～をします」と、一時的活動を言うときの「(今)～をしています」の違いについて理解し、使い分けができるようにしましょう。

■ Vocabulary 英語の意味を下の日本語から選びましょう。 🔘 1-41

1. to take a nap (　)　　2. dormitory (　)　　3. strict (　)　　4. abroad (　)

5. bilingual (　)　　　6. fluent (　)　　　7. to conduct (　)

8. as well as ~ (　)　　9. offer (　)　　　10. apart from ~ (　)

---

a. 提供する　　b. 流ちょうな　　c. 厳しい　　d. 行う　　e. 海外に

f. ～だけでなく　　g. 寮　　h. いねむりをする　　i. ～を別にすれば　　j. 二か国語を話す人

■ Warm-up : Students' Activities

CDを聞いて、それぞれのイラストの説明として正しければ○、誤っていれば×を□の中に書きましょう。 🔘 1-42

1.  □

2.  □

3.  □

4.  □

5.  □

6.  □

もう一度CDを聞き、下の（　）を埋めて、答えを確認しましょう。　repeat　CD 1-42

1. A woman (　　　　　　) (　　　　　　) (　　　　　　　) a crowded train.

2. Two students (　　　　　) (　　　　　) at a table.

3. A student (　　　　　) (　　　　　) a notebook.

4. Some students (　　　　　　) (　　　　　　) an exam.

5. A girl (　　　　　) (　　　　　) on the phone.

6. He (　　　　　) (　　　　　　) part-time at a gas station.

▮ Grammar Point ：進行形（現在進行形、過去進行形）
＜be動詞＋〜ing＞で「（…を）している」を表す

▶現在形が、現在の状態や習慣的な動作・できごとを表すのに対して、現在進行形は、「今」進行中あるいは一時的に継続中の動作・できごとを表します。

	現在形	現在進行形
肯定文	I use a computer every day. 私は毎日コンピュータを使う。	I am using a computer now. 私は今コンピュータを使っている。
	Ken always studies hard. ケンはいつも一生懸命勉強する。	Ken is studying hard these days. ケンは近頃一生懸命勉強している。
疑問文	Do you use a computer every day? あなたは毎日コンピュータを使いますか。	Are you using a computer now? あなたは今コンピュータを使っていますか。
否定文	I don't use a computer every day. 私は毎日はコンピュータを使わない。	I am not using a computer now. 私は今コンピュータを使っていない。

▶同様に、過去形が、過去の状態や（習慣的な）動作・できごとを表すのに対して、過去進行形は、「その時」進行中（あるいは一時的に継続中）の動作・できごとを表します。

	過去形	過去進行形
肯定文	I used a computer yesterday. 私は昨日コンピュータを使った。	I was using a computer then. 私はその時コンピュータを使っていた。
	They took a test last week. 彼らは先週テストを受けた。	They were taking a test at that time. 彼らはその時テストを受けていた。
疑問文	Did you use a computer yesterday? あなたは昨日コンピュータを使いましたか。	Were you using a computer then? あなたはその時コンピュータを使っていましたか。
否定文	I didn't use a computer yesterday. 私は昨日コンピュータを使わなかった。	I wasn't using a computer then. 私はその時コンピュータを使っていなかった。

Grammar Practice

A. （　）内の語を正しい形にして下線部に書きましょう。

1. It _____ hard at that time. (snow)

2. I usually _____ to school by bus. (go)

3. My brother is a teacher, but he _____ lessons right now.
   (not, give)

4. Look at Tom. He _____ a nap in class. (take)

5. Peter is very good at languages. He _____ five languages very well. (speak)

B. 選択肢の中で最も適切なものを選び、1〜5の英文を完成させましょう。

1. Tomoko _____ a radio English course every morning.
   (A) is listening to   (B) listens   (C) listened   (D) listens to

2. Students often _____ in college dormitories.
   (A) live   (B) have lived   (C) lives   (D) are living

3. Look at the picture. That strict teacher _____.
   (A) smiles   (B) is smiling   (C) smiled   (D) are smiling

4. John couldn't answer the phone then. He _____ a bath.
   (A) took   (B) was taking   (C) is taking   (D) has taken

5. Could you turn the light on? It _____ dark.
   (A) was getting   (B) is getting   (C) gets   (D) got

■ Dialogue

文末の日本語を参考にして対話文の（　　）に適語を入れましょう。その後で、CDを聞いて
答えを確認し、ペアで対話練習をしましょう。 (CD) 1-43

Julie happens to meet Ken on the street.

Julie: Hi, Ken. What (　　　　　) you (　　　　　) here? ［している］

Ken: I (　　　　) (　　　　　) for Sho. ［待っている］

      We promised to meet here.

Julie: I saw him at the next corner. He (　　　　　) (　　　　　) to call

      somebody. ［〜しようとして（試みて）いた］

Ken: Ah, I think he (　　　　) (　　　　　) me. ［電話をしていた］ I left my

      phone at home.

Julie: I hope he (　　　　) still (　　　　　) there. ［立っている］

Ken: I'll go and find him. Thank you.

Let's check some more!

● 基本的に、動作や行為を表す動詞は進行形にできますが、状態や感情、知覚を表す動詞
は進行形にできません。

● 近い未来の予定を表すのに現在進行形を使うこともあります。
（例）I am leaving for Paris tonight.（今晩パリにたつ予定だ。）
（例）He is coming back from America next Sunday.（彼は日曜日にアメリカか
　　ら帰国する予定だ。）

▌Reading : *Studying Abroad* 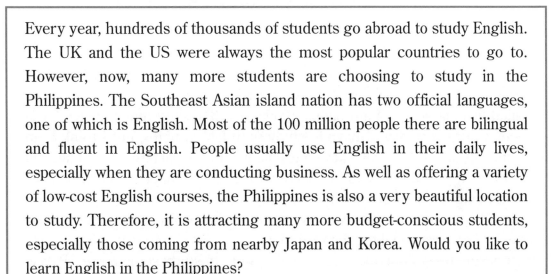 1-44

Every year, hundreds of thousands of students go abroad to study English. The UK and the US were always the most popular countries to go to. However, now, many more students are choosing to study in the Philippines. The Southeast Asian island nation has two official languages, one of which is English. Most of the 100 million people there are bilingual and fluent in English. People usually use English in their daily lives, especially when they are conducting business. As well as offering a variety of low-cost English courses, the Philippines is also a very beautiful location to study. Therefore, it is attracting many more budget-conscious students, especially those coming from nearby Japan and Korea. Would you like to learn English in the Philippines?

budget-conscious 予算を気にする

A. 文中の現在進行形の部分に下線を引きましょう。

B. 質問文を読んで英語で答えましょう。

1. What were the most popular countries for students to study English in?

2. How many official languages does the Philippines have?

3. Apart from in their daily lives, in which situation are most people using English?

4. What are the good points of studying English in the Philippines?

5. Which countries' students is the Philippines mainly attracting?

■ Writing

A. ペンフレンドのNickがShoに宛てた手紙を読みましょう。　1-45

Dear Sho,

How are you? How are you doing at college? I am sorry that I couldn't write to you sooner. A lot of things are happening in my life. Last year I failed two classes, so I am taking 10 classes this semester. I have a lot of homework every day. I have to study until late at night, but I think I am doing OK at school. I also have a problem with my part-time job. I am still working at McDonald's, and I quarreled with the manager yesterday. Now I am thinking about quitting the job. My band members know some other good jobs. By the way, we are going to have our first concert next week. I am really looking forward to it.

I have a test tomorrow, so now I am going to study some more. Please let me know how you are getting along.

All the best,

Nick

B. Shoになったつもりで、Nickに近況を伝える手紙を書いてみましょう。できるだけ現在進行形を使ってみましょう。

_____

_____

_____

_____

_____

_____

_____

_____

_____

_____

_____

_____

_____

54

On Vacation 未来表現

バケーション（休暇）は、英語圏でもしばしば話題にのぼります。このユニットでは、休暇をどう過ごすかなど、未来の予定について述べる練習をしましょう。

■ Vocabulary 英語の意味を下の日本語から選びましょう。 🎵 1-46

1. hometown (　)　2. to work part-time (　)　3. to save (　)
4. to join (　)　5. a couple of (　)　6. volunteer (　)　7. basic (　)
8. local (　)　9. sightseeing (　)　10. deadline (　)

a. 締切り	b. 参加する	c. 故郷	d. 2つの	e. アルバイトをする
f. 地元の	g. 有志	h. 基礎的な	i. 貯金する	j. 観光

■ Warm-up : The Summer Vacation

CDを聞き、4人の人物の夏休みの予定をボックスの1と2から1つずつ選んで、アルファベットを□に書きましょう。 🎵 1-47

1	a. go back to his/her hometown　　b. go to summer school c. go to Australia　　　　d. work part-time
2	e. save money　　f. stay for one month　　g. study English h. stay at his/her uncle's house

Ken 　□ □

Sho 　□ □

Hiroshi 　□ □

Mari 　□ □

もう一度CDを聞き、下の（　）を埋めて、答えを確認しましょう。 **repeat** 🎧 CD 1-47

Hi, I'm Ken.　The summer vacation is coming soon.　Everyone around me is talking about the summer vacation.　My best friend, Sho, is going to (¹　　　　) a trip to Australia.　He is going to (²　　　　　) at his uncle's house.　Another friend, Hiroshi, is going back to his hometown.　I think he (³　　　　　) (⁴　　　　　) there for one month.　My sister, Mari, is planning to go to a summer school.　She is going to (⁵　　　　) English very hard.　Me?　I'm not sure yet.　I want to go abroad, but I don't have much money.　Hmm. . .　Well, I (⁶　　　　) probably (⁷　　　　) part-time and (⁸　　　　) money!　So, what (⁹　　　　) you (¹⁰　　　　) (¹¹　　　　) (¹²　　　　) this summer?

■ Grammar Point : 未来表現 (be going to, will)

▶「～だろう」、「～するつもりだ」、「～しよう」など未来のことを表すには主に be going to と will を使います。

▶be going to と will は、同じ意味で使う場合と、使い分けが必要な場合があります。

単純な未来の予測 be going to will （基本的に同じ意味）	主語	be going to will	動詞の原形
	Ken Ken	is going to will	go to the movies tomorrow. go to the movies tomorrow.
	ケンは明日映画に行くでしょう。		
すでに予定した意図や、確実に起こりそうな未来の予測 be going to	主語	be going to	動詞の原形
	I	am going to	go to Australia next month.
	私は来月オーストラリアに行きます。（既に計画を立てている）		
	It	is going to	rain.
	雨が降りそうだ。（状況から確実に起こりそうである）		
その場で決めた意思 will	主語	will	動詞の原形
	I	will	go to the movies tomorrow.
	明日は映画に行こう。（その場で決めた）		

▶willを使った文の疑問文と否定文

疑問文	Will	主語	動詞の原形
	Will	she	go to Okinawa this summer?
否定文	主語	will not (won't)	動詞の原形
	She	will not (won't)	come back until next week.

■ Grammar Practice

A. ( ) 内の語を並べ替えて、意味の通る英文にしましょう。

1. (tennis, Tom, to, play, is, next, going) weekend.

_____

2. (travel, to, are, in, we, Thailand, going) during the vacation.

_____

3. (Japan, come, he, will, to, back, when) next?

_____

4. (going, get, are, to, there, how, you)?

_____

5. (home, are, to, be, at, going, not, they) during the holidays.

_____

B. 選択肢の中で最も適切なものを選び、1〜5の英文を完成させましょう。

1. My father _____ going to join our trip. He is too busy.
   (A) is   (B) are   (C) isn't   (D) will

2. There _____ be a lot of people in Kyoto during the holidays.
   (A) is   (B) are   (C) will   (D) going

3. What shall I do this weekend? Well, I _____ probably go to the movies.
   (A) am   (B) do   (C) will   (D) going

4. What time _____ the plane arrive?

(A) is   (B) will   (C) do   (D) going

5. He _____ come back from Australia in a couple of weeks.

(A) will be   (B) is going   (C) has   (D) is going to

▎Dialogue

対話文を聞いた後、ペアで ☐ の部分を入れ替えて練習しましょう。最後は、☐ の部分を自分で考えて対話練習しましょう。 (CD) 1-48

Lillian and Ken are talking about the weekend.

Lillian: What are you going to do this weekend?

Ken: I am going to ☐ play beach volleyball ☐ .¹

Lillian: Really? Did you know there is going to be a typhoon?

Ken: What? Then I'll ☐ call my friends and play in the gym ☐ ² instead.

Lillian: Good idea.

	1. 屋外のアクティビティ	2. 屋内のアクティビティ
対話 ①	have a barbecue at the riverside	invite my friend to go to the movies
対話 ②	go hiking in the country	stay at home and watch a DVD
対話 ③	go to a theme park	stay at home and play computer games

Let's check some more!

● be going to の否定文と疑問文は、通常の be 動詞の場合と同じです。

(例) He isn't going to travel this summer. (彼はこの夏は旅行しないだろう。)

(例) Are you going to stay at that expensive hotel?

(あの高いホテルに泊まるのですか？)

● 進行形で確定している未来を表すことができます。

(例) I'm going to Thailand. (タイに行きます。)

I am Yukiko. I am a college student. I am going to take a vacation as a volunteer this summer. I am going to Thailand to teach Japanese and basic math to children. I am going to teach at school in the morning, and then I will have free time in the afternoon. Maybe I will learn some Thai culture, such as Thai language, dance, and cooking from local people. I am especially interested in Thai cooking because I really like spicy food. There will also be other volunteers from different countries. I am very excited because I like meeting new people. I will communicate with them in English, so my English will improve. I am worried about just one thing. It will be very hot and rain a lot in Thailand! Anyway, it will be a great experience for me.

A. 文中から未来表現の be going to と will を見つけて下線を引きましょう。

B. 次の文が英文の内容と合っていればT、合っていなければFと書きましょう。

1. Yukiko is going to go to Thailand for sightseeing. ( )

2. She is going to teach English to children. ( )

3. She is interested in Thai culture. ( )

4. There will be other foreign volunteers. ( )

5. She is worried about Thai food. ( )

 **Writing**

A. 以下は、留学生との交流を目的としたバーベキュー・パーティーのお知らせです。これを読んで、催し物の概要を表（Table 1）にまとめましょう。 ((CD)) 1-50

Barbecue Party with International Students!

We are going to have a barbecue with international students on Enoshima beach on Sunday, August 1. We will meet at Enoshima Station (on the Enoshima Line) at 10 a.m. All the food will be taken care of. The cost will be 1,500 yen per person. You'll need to bring your own drinks. We are going to play beach volleyball after the barbecue lunch. Don't forget to bring your swimsuit. The deadline for signing up is Monday, July 26.

Table 1 Barbecue	
Date	
Place	
Meeting place	
Cost	
Things to bring	
Deadline for sign-up	

Table 2	
Date	
Place	
Meeting place	
Cost	
Things to bring	
Deadline for sign-up	

B. 次に、表（Table 1）を参考にして、別の催し物（例：クリスマス・パーティー、ハロウィーン・パーティー、ピクニック、キャンプ等）を考えて概要を表（Table 2）に記入してみましょう。そして、この表をもとに、その催し物についての案内文を英語で書きましょう。

Out and About 助動詞 (1)

私たちは、日々いろいろな場所で、様々な人々と会話を交わしています。コミュニケーションを円滑に進めるために、知っておくと便利な助動詞について学習しましょう。

■ Vocabulary 英語の意味を下の日本語から選びましょう。 🎵 1-51

1. to hold on ( )　　2. on another line ( )　　3. professor ( )

4. to lend ( )　　5. excellent ( )　　6. mall ( )　　7. in addition ( )

8. theme park ( )　　9. polite ( )　　　10. against the law ( )

a. ショッピングセンター	b. 法に反する	c. 貸す	d. 電話を切らないでおく
e. 教授　　f. 電話中	g. すぐれた	h. テーマパーク	i. その上　　j. 礼儀正しい

■ Warm-up : Common Expressions

下の6つの場所ではどんな英語表現が使われそうですか？アルファベットを□に書きましょう。

a. May I come in?	b. Can I smoke at this table?
c. I can't see the screen.	d. Would you hold on a minute?
e. He can play the piano really well.	f. Could you lend me your dictionary?

1. On the phone □

2. At a movie theater □

3. Outside a professor's office □

4. In a restaurant □

5. In a classroom □

6. At a concert hall □

 CDを聞いて、答えをチェックしましょう。 🎵 1-52

もう一度CDを聞き、下の (　) を埋めて、答えを確認しましょう。　repeat　(CD) 1-52

1.　A: (　　　　　　　　) you hold on a minute? He is on another line now.

　　B:　No problem.

2.　A: The man in front is too tall. I (　　　　　　) see the screen.

　　B: Let's change seats then.

3.　A: Professor Craig, (　　　　　　) I come in?

　　B: Certainly, please come in.

4.　A: (　　　　　　) I smoke at this table?

　　B: I'm sorry, sir, but this is a non-smoking table.

5.　A: (　　　　　　) you lend me your dictionary?

　　B: Sure, no problem.

6.　A: He (　　　　　　) play the piano really well.

　　B: Yes. He's an excellent player.

▰ Grammar Point：助動詞 (1) can, may など

▶助動詞は、動詞(原形)の前に置いて、動詞に意味を加える働きをします。

▶肯定文、疑問文、否定文の作り方

肯定文	助動詞の後に動詞の原形	I can speak English. 私は英語を話すことができる。
疑問文	助動詞が文頭	Can you speak English？ あなたは英語を話すことができますか。
否定文	助動詞の後に not	I cannot (can't) speak English. 私は英語を話すことができない。

▶能力・許可・依頼を表す助動詞

能力 〜することができる	I can play the piano. I can't see the screen.
許可 〜してよい 〜してよいですか	You can use my pen. Can I smoke here? Could I take your photo?（*canより丁寧） May I come in?（*canより丁寧）
依頼 〜してくれますか	Can you help me? Could you lend me your dictionary?（*Can you〜?より丁寧） Will you close the door? Would you hold on a minute?（*Will you〜?より丁寧）
申し出	May I help you? Would you like a cup of tea?

Grammar Practice

A. （　　）内の語句を並べ替えて、意味の通る英文にしましょう。

1. (you, me, pass, the salt, could), please?

   _____

2. (toilet, I, may, use, the)?

   _____

3. (can't, my, I, find, glasses).

   _____

4. (have, address, your, can, I)?

   _____

5. (you, back, me, would, call) later ?

   _____

B. 選択肢の中で最も適切なものを選び、1〜5の英文を完成させましょう。

1. It's getting cold here. _____ please close the window?
    (A) May I   (B) Would you   (C) Have you   (D) Could I

2. I _____ believe the prices in that store!
    (A) may   (B) wouldn't   (C) can't   (D) can

3. Could _____ tell me how to get to the station?
    (A) you   (B) I   (C) me   (D) it

4. Yesterday's class was very difficult, and I _____ understand the teacher.
    (A) can't   (B) wouldn't   (C) may   (D) couldn't

5. Hello. This is John Black. _____ speak to Mr. Smith?
    (A) Will you   (B) May I   (C) Can you   (D) Would you

■ Dialogue

対話文を聞いた後、ペアで ☐ の部分を入れ替えて練習しましょう。最後は、 ☐ の部分を自分で考えて対話練習しましょう。 (CD) 1-53

A waiter welcomes a customer at a restaurant.

Waiter: Welcome. Would you like a smoking or non-smoking seat?

Customer: Non-smoking please. . . Could I sit next to the window ?[1]

Waiter: Yes, of course.

Customer: And can I have the menu, please ?[2]

	1. 要望 ①	2. 要望 ②
対話 ①	have a seat in the corner	have a glass of water, please
対話 ②	sit at the counter	have some ice in the glass, please
対話 ③	sit on the terrace	borrow a blanket, please

Let's check some more!

● canはbe able toに置き換えられる場合もあります。
● canには完了形や未来表現がないので、be able toを代わりに使います。
　(例) Nobody has been able to defeat the champion.
　(例) You will be able to speak English fluently if you practice.

Reading : *The Mall of America* 1-54

The Mall of America is located in Minnesota, USA. It is a very, very big shopping mall. It has 520 shops and 40 million visitors every year. You can do many things in the mall. Of course, you can shop and eat. In addition, you can visit a theme park and even get married at a wedding chapel. You can also meet one of the 12,000 workers, and he or she will probably ask, "May I help you?" or "Would you like some help?" Shop workers in the USA are polite. However, you can't smoke in the mall's restaurants and bars because it is against the law in Minnesota. Do you like shopping? Why don't you visit the Mall of America?

A. 文中の助動詞に下線を引き、それぞれの意味を考えましょう。

B. 質問文を読んで英語で答えましょう。

1. Where is the Mall of America?

   _____

2. How many shops are there in the mall?

   _____

3. What can you do in the Mall of America? Write four things.

   _____

4. What will the mall's workers ask you?

   _____

5. What can't you do in the mall?

   _____

◼ Writing

それぞれの状況下で、あなただったらどのような英語表現を使いますか？
空欄を埋めてみましょう。

---

1. *You have just sat down in a restaurant. You want to see a menu.*

   _____

   _____

   _____ menu?

---

2. *You want to buy a ticket for a movie.*

   _____

   _____

   _____ for *Aladdin,* please?

---

3. *You have just paid a taxi driver. You need a receipt.*

   _____

   _____

   _____ receipt, please?

---

4. *Your friend looks thirsty.*

   _____

   _____

   _____ a glass of water?

---

5. *You want to know the time. You ask a passerby.*

   _____

   _____

   _____ time, please?

---

6. *You want your friend to call you tomorrow.*

   _____

   _____

   _____ tomorrow, please?

Rules 助動詞 (2)

世の中には様々な決まり事があります。法律であったり、しきたりであったり、お互いに嫌な思いをせずに暮らしていくために必要なものです。このユニットでは、決まり事を相手に尋ねたり伝えたりするときによく使う助動詞について学びましょう。

Vocabulary 英語の意味を下の日本語から選びましょう。 2-01

1. to reduce (　)　　2. to recycle (　)　　3. product (　)
4. to disturb (　)　　5. traffic light (　)　　6. to take off (　)
7. to quit (　)　　8. government (　)　　9. founder (　)
10. to behave (　)

a. 脱ぐ、はずす　　b. 妨げる、迷惑をかける　　c. ふるまう　　d. 再利用する
e. 製品　　f. 政府　　g. 減らす　　h. 創立者　　i. 信号　　j. やめる、中止する

Warm-up : Signs

それぞれの標識や表示の表す意味を下のボックスから選んで、アルファベットを□に書きましょう。

a. You should not cross the road.　　b. You must stop here.
c. You can park here.　　d. You cannot use your smartphone here.
e. You must reduce your speed.　　f. You should recycle this product.

1. □
2. □
3. □
4. □
5. □
6. □

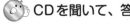 CDを聞いて、答えをチェックしましょう。 2-02

もう一度CDを聞き、下の (　) を埋めて、答えを確認しましょう。　repeat　CD 2-02

1. The three-arrow sign means you (　　　　　　) try to recycle most products; especially paper, plastic, and glass.

2. You (　　　　　) use your smartphone in the classroom because it (　　　　　) disturb other students.

3. You (　　　　　) reduce your speed at a slow sign because it is dangerous to go fast.

4. You (　　　　　) (　　　　　　) cross the road when the traffic light is yellow.

5. You (　　　　　) stop at a stop sign. It is not possible to go further.

6. A 'P' means that you (　　　　　) park in this place although you may (　　　　) (　　　　) pay.

█ Grammar Point：助動詞 (2) must, should など

▶義務・必要・忠告を表す助動詞

義務 必要	～しなければならない	You must stop here. You have to wear a tie at work.
	～する必要はない	You don't have to work on Saturdays.
禁止	～してはならない	You must not (mustn't) play with matches. You cannot (can't) eat in this taxi.
忠告	～したほうがいい ～すべきである	You should recycle this product. You had better hurry up. *shouldより命令的
	～しないほうがいい ～すべきでない	You should not (shouldn't) touch the animals. You had better not be late.

▶推量を表す助動詞

推量	～かもしれない	It may snow tonight. He might be in his office.
	～ではないかもしれない	The news may not be true. She might not know the news.

68

▮ Grammar Practice

A. [　] の日本語の意味にあてはまる助動詞を使って英文を完成させましょう。すべて、You. . .で始めましょう。

1. smoke on trains in Japan. 〔～してはならない〕

_____

2. wear warm clothes when you climb Mt. Fuji. 〔～した方がいい〕

_____

3. pass a difficult test to enter this university. 〔～しなければならない〕

_____

4. drive until you are 18 years old. 〔～してはならない〕

_____

5. use your smartphone in class. 〔～すべきでない〕

_____

B. 選択肢の中で最も適切なものを選び、1～5の英文を完成させましょう。

1. You are always late. You _____ come to class earlier.
    (A) are   (B) must not   (C) had better   (D) cannot

2. You _____ drink bottled water when you travel abroad.
    (A) should   (B) had better not (C) cannot   (D) don't have to

3. My doctor said that I _____ quit smoking.
    (A) did   (B) should   (C) shouldn't   (D) had better not

4. I have an English test tomorrow. I _____ study tonight.
    (A) can   (B) must not   (C) have   (D) have to

5. You _____ stay here if you don't follow the rules.
    (A) can   (B) may   (C) cannot   (D) wouldn't

▐ Dialogue

対話文を聞いた後、ペアで ☐ の部分を入れ替えて練習しましょう。最後は、☐ の部分を自分で考えて対話練習しましょう。 🔘 2-03

Jason and Miki are talking about Japanese rules.

Jason: What should I do when I | visit someone's home |¹ in Japan?

Miki: First, you must | take off your shoes at the entrance |.²

Jason: OK, and what else?

Miki: You should | bring some small gifts like chocolates or tea |.³

	1. 状況	2. 忠告	3. 忠告
対話 ①	sit down to eat	say "itadakimasu"	use chopsticks, if you can
対話 ②	take a bath	shower before getting in the bath	not take your towel into the bath
対話 ③	visit a shrine	behave calmly in the shrine	bring some small coins

---

Let's check some more!

● mustとhave toは通常同じ意味で使用されますが、微妙にニュアンスが違うときがあります。例えば、社会的状況（客観的状況）から「しなければならない」ときは、have toを使用し、自分の判断から「しなければならない」ときは、mustを使います。

Reading : *An Unusual School* 2-04

I love this school.

Summerhill School in southern England is different from normal schools. Students at the school have a lot of choices in their education. They don't have to attend classes and they can choose what to do with their time. This means that the school sometimes has trouble with the government. They think that all students must attend classes. However, the founder of Summerhill, A.S. Neill said that children should choose to live their own life. They shouldn't listen to their parents or the government. He believed that children should make their own rules. Therefore, there is a meeting every week at the school when the students can change or make school rules. One rule the students made was about stealing; the thief has to pay the money back to the victim. Most students are very happy with this kind of system. Is this the kind of school you would like to go to?

victim 被害者

A. 文中の助動詞に下線を引き、それぞれの意味を考えましょう。

B. 次の文が英文の内容と合っていればT、合っていなければFと書きましょう。

1. Summerhill is in England. ( )

2. Summerhill is a normal school. ( )

3. Students have to attend classes. ( )

4. The school sometimes has trouble with the government. ( )

5. The students make their own rules. ( )

Writing

A. 次の5つはミカが心に決めた事です。 2-05

> **Personal Rules**
> 1. I must not be late for school.
> 2. I must clean my room every day.
> 3. I should practice listening to English more often.
> 4. I can eat chocolate only on weekends.
> 5. I must call my mother once a week.

B. Aを参考にして、自分が心に決めた事を5つ書きましょう。

1. _____

2. _____

3. _____

4. _____

5. _____

Folk Tales 接続詞 (1)

このユニットでは昔話やおとぎ話を題材にして、語と語、句と句、節と節などを対等の関係で結びつける等位接続詞（and, but, or, soなど）の使い方を学びましょう。

■ Vocabulary 英語の意味を下の日本語から選びましょう。 🔘 2-06

1. bridegroom ( )　　2. to shine ( )　　3. thus ( )　　4. mean ( )
5. to fall asleep ( )　6. to leave ( )　　7. to bind ( )
8. to set ~ free ( )　9. to gather ( )　　10. store ( )

a. だから	b. 集める	c. 意地悪な	d. 輝く、光る	e. 縛る
f. 花婿	g. 別れる、出発する	h. ~を自由にする	i. 蓄え	j. 眠りに落ちる

■ Warm-up : The Marriage of the Mouse Girl

CDを聞き、話の順番に□に番号を入れましょう。 🔘 2-07

A.　　　　　B.　　　　　C.

□　　　　　□　　　　　□

D.　　　　　E.　　　　　F.

□　　　　　□　　　　　□

もう一度CDを聞き、下の（　）を埋めて、答えを確認しましょう。　**repeat** CD 2-07

Long, long ago, there was a beautiful mouse girl. Her father (1   ) mother wanted to find the most wonderful bridegroom in the world for their daughter. The father said, "The sun shines (2   ) gives us light, (3   ) I think he is the best man." The parents went to the sun (4   ) asked him to marry their daughter. The sun was pleased (5   ) said, "The cloud sometimes hides me, (6   ) he may be stronger than me. Who do you prefer, me (7   ) the cloud?" They decided to ask the cloud next. The cloud said, "The wind blows me away, (8   ) he is stronger than me." They went to ask the wind next, (9   ) he was not the best man. He said, "The wall is stronger. It stops me." Then they went to the wall, (10   ) the wall said, "The mouse is strong (11   ) eats me." Thus, finally they decided to make their daughter marry a handsome mouse. The young couple got married (12   ) lived happily ever after.

▰ **Grammar Point**：等位接続詞 (and, but, or, so)

▶語、句、節などを対等の関係で結ぶのが（等位）接続詞です。主なものはand, but, or, soです。

and 〜と〜 そして	The country mouse and the town mouse were very good friends. 田舎のねずみと都会のねずみはとても仲良しでした。
	Cinderella married the prince, and they lived happily ever after. シンデレラは王子様と結婚し、（そして）二人はずっと幸せに暮らしました。
but しかし	The old man was very kind, but his wife was mean. おじいさんはとても親切でしたが、（しかし）おばあさんは意地悪でした。
or 〜か〜 あるいは	Which is stronger, the sun or the north wind? 太陽か北風か、どちらがより強いですか？
	Do you want to be rich, or do you want to stay poor? 金持ちになりたいかい、それとも貧乏のままでいいのかい？
so だから そこで	Snow White was very tired, so she fell asleep in the bed. 白雪姫はとても疲れていたので、ベッドで眠りこんでしまいました。

74

▶ 「命令文＋and」「命令文＋or」は、それぞれ次のような意味になります。

命令文＋and ～しなさい、 そうすれば…	Come to my home in town, and you'll be able to try a lot of delicious food. 町の僕の家へおいでよ、そうすればご馳走がいっぱい食べられるよ。
命令文＋or ～しなさい、 さもないと…	Keep it secret, or I'll have to leave you. 秘密を守ってください、さもないとお別れしなければなりません。

■ Grammar Practice

A. 「ライオンとねずみ」という話です。（　　）内の語句を並べ替えて、意味の通る英文にしましょう。

One day, a lion found a mouse moving on his back.

1. The lion was hungry, (caught, the, mouse, so, he) to eat.

   The lion was hungry, _____ to eat.

2. The mouse said, "Let me go, (you, will, help, I, and) some day."

   The mouse said, "Let me go, _____ some day."

3. The lion didn't believe it, (the mouse, he, let, but, go).

   The lion didn't believe it, _____.

4. A few days later, some hunters caught the lion (a tree, him, to, and, bound).

   A few days later, some hunters caught the lion _____.

5. The mouse showed up (free, and, lion, the, set) by biting the ropes.

   The mouse showed up _____ by biting the ropes.

B. 選択肢の中で最も適切なものを選び、1～5の英文を完成させましょう。

1. The dog said to Momotaro, "Give me one of your dumplings, (　　　　) I will follow you."

   (A) and　　　　(B) but　　　　(C) or　　　　(D) so

2. The sparrow said, "Would you like this big box, (　　　　) would you like that small box?"

   (A) for　　　　(B) but　　　　(C) or　　　　(D) so

3. The wolf tried to blow the brick house down, (　　　　) he couldn't.

   (A) and   (B) but   (C) or   (D) so

4. The monster said to the boy, "Tell me the secret, (　　　　) I will kill you."

   (A) and   (B) but   (C) or   (D) so

5. Kaguya Hime was very beautiful, (　　　　) many men wanted to marry her.

   (A) for   (B) but   (C) or   (D) so

■ Dialogue

(　) に and, but, or, so のいずれかを入れて対話文を完成させましょう。その後に CD を聞いて答えを確認し、最後にペアで対話文を練習しましょう。　🄲 2-08

Ken and Mary meet in the library.

Ken:　Hi, Mary.　Are you free to go to the movies tonight?

Mary: I'm sorry, Ken.　I have a test tomorrow, (　　　　) I have to study.

Ken:　OK, (　　　) let's try to go on Saturday (　　　　) Sunday.

Mary: Sure.　Come to the library tomorrow, (　　　　) we'll decide then.

◼ **Reading** : *The Cricket and the Ants* ◎ 2-09

The winter began, (① and / or) the cricket was very hungry. He heard that the ants had a great store of food, (② so / but) the cricket went to the ants' house. He begged for some food, (③ so / but) all the ants shook their heads. Finally one of them spoke. "We were all busy gathering food during the hot summer. Why didn't you help us?" "I was so busy singing every day," said the cricket. "You are tired of singing now, aren't you?" "Oh, yes, I sang too much." "So, why don't you dance now?" said the ant, closing the door.

cricket コオロギ（キリギリス）　**beg for** 〜を求める

A. 文中の (　　) の中から適語を選びましょう。

B. 次の文が英文の内容と合っていればT、合っていなければFと書きましょう。

1. The cricket wanted to get some food from the ants.　　　　　　　(　　)

2. The cricket didn't work during the summer.　　　　　　　　　　(　　)

3. Now the cricket does not want to sing any more.　　　　　　　　(　　)

4. The ants wanted to see the cricket dance.　　　　　　　　　　　(　　)

5. The ants didn't give the cricket any food.　　　　　　　　　　　(　　)

▰ Writing

A. 以下の「浦島太郎」の話を読んでみましょう。 (CD) 2-10

Long, long ago, there lived a fisherman named Urashima Taro. One day Taro was walking on the beach and saw some children tormenting a turtle. Taro saved the turtle from the children. A few days later, the turtle came back to Taro and said, "Thank you for saving me. Today I will take you to the Dragon Palace." The turtle took Taro on his back to the Dragon Palace under the sea. Taro met a beautiful princess named Otohime there. Taro ate delicious food and enjoyed singing and dancing with her every day. Life in the palace was like a dream, so he totally forgot his old life.

Three years passed, and suddenly Taro remembered his old mother and his hometown. He said good-bye to Otohime. Then she gave him a little box as a gift and said, "This is a magic box called Tamatebako. You can open it when you are in trouble." Taro went back to his hometown, but he could find neither his mother nor his old house. Taro was at a loss, so he opened the Tamatebako. Then some white smoke came out, and Taro suddenly became an old man with a long white beard.

....

torment いじめる　**at a loss** 途方に暮れる

B. 「浦島太郎」の話を参考にして、グループで協力しあって、自分たちの知っている昔話や話のあらすじを書きましょう。その際にand, but, or, soなどを使ってみましょう。

_____

_____

_____

_____

_____

_____

_____

_____

_____

News & Events 受動態

テレビや新聞で報道される内容は、受け身の形つまり受動態で表されることがよくあります。このユニットでは、過去から現在の様々なニュースや出来事を通して、受動態の使い方を学びましょう。

■ Vocabulary 英語の意味を下の日本語から選びましょう。 ⊚ 2-11

1. to invent (　)　2. to hold (　)　　3. to destroy (　)　4. to sink (　)
5. to award (　)　6. scholarship (　)　7. awful (　)　　8. token (　)
9. ambassador (　)　10. jewelry (　)

a. 行う	b. ひどい	c. 沈める	d. しるし	e. 授与する
f. 奨学金	g. 大使	h. 破壊する	i. 発明する	j. 宝石類

■ Warm-up : Do You Know When. . . ?

6つの出来事と時間表現を組み合わせてみましょう。□にアルファベットを書きましょう。

a. in 1903	b. in 1912	c. every four years
d. every year	e. in 1997	f. in 2001

1. Nobel Prizes given ☐

2. Princess Diana killed ☐

3. The airplane invented ☐

4. The Summer Olympics held ☐

5. The World Trade Center destroyed ☐

6. The Titanic sunk ☐

 CDを聞いて、答えをチェックしましょう。 2-12

もう一度CDを度聞き、下の(　)を埋めて、答えを確認しましょう。 **repeat** 🔘 2-12

1. Nobel Prizes (　　　　　　) (　　　　　　　　　) every year.

2. Princess Diana (　　　　　　) (　　　　　　　　　) in a car accident in 1997.

3. The airplane (　　　　　　) (　　　　　　　) by the Wright Brothers in 1903.

4. The summer Olympic Games (　　　　　　) (　　　　　　) every four years.

5. The World Trade Center (　　　　　) (　　　　　　) by terrorists in 2001.

6. The *Titanic* (　　　　　　) (　　　　　　) by an iceberg in 1912.

■ Grammar Point：受動態

<be動詞＋過去分詞>で「〜は…される」を表す

▶受動態の作り方

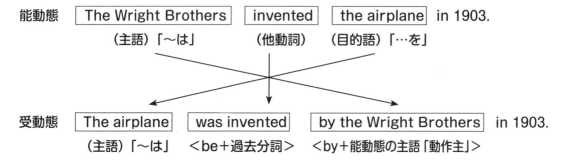

能動態　The Wright Brothers　invented　the airplane　in 1903.
　　　　（主語）「〜は」　　（他動詞）　（目的語）「…を」

受動態　The airplane　was invented　by the Wright Brothers　in 1903.
　　　　（主語）「〜は」　<be＋過去分詞>　<by＋能動態の主語「動作主」>

▶受動態が使われるのは以下のような場合です。

話題の焦点が（動作主よりも）動作を受ける方にある	The World Trade Center was destroyed by terrorists. 世界貿易センターはテロリストによって破壊された。
	The Harry Potter books were written by J.K. Rowling. ハリー・ポッターの本はJ.K.Rowlingによって書かれた。
動作主を特定する必要がない by〜が省略される	Nobel Prizes are given every year. ノーベル賞は毎年授与される。
	French is spoken in many African countries. フランス語は多くのアフリカ諸国で話される。
慣用表現 状態や感情を表すものが多い。by以外の前置詞が使用される	The ground is covered with snow. 地面は雪で覆われている。
	The teacher is known to every student. その先生は全ての生徒に知られている。

Grammar Practice

A. 次の文を受動態に変えましょう。

1. Many people visit Tokyo Disney Resort every year.

   →_____ every year.

2. Machiko Hasegawa wrote *Sazae-san*.

   →_____.

3. Bell invented the telephone in the 19th century.

   →_____ in the 19th century.

4. In 1997, Japan hosted an international meeting in Kyoto.

   →In 1997, _____.

5. They sell popular CDs at the store.

   →_____.

B. 選択肢の中で最も適切なものを選び、1〜5の英文を完成させましょう。

1. The window _____ by the baseball.
   (A) break   (B) has broken   (C) was broken   (D) broke

2. Our meals _____ by our grandmother.
   (A) prepared   (B) was prepared   (C) are preparing   (D) are prepared

3. English and French _____ in many countries in Africa.
   (A) have spoken   (B) are spoken   (C) are speaking   (D) is spoken

4. Some good weather _____ this weekend.
   (A) expects   (B) expected   (C) will expect   (D) is expected

5. I _____ in Japan, but I grew up in the U.S.
   (A) am born   (B) was born   (C) bore   (D) born

◾ Dialogue

対話文を聞いた後、ペアで ☐ の部分を入れ替えて練習しましょう。最後は、 ☐ の部分を自分で考えて対話練習しましょう。 (CD) 2-13

Jeff and Mariko meet before class.

Jeff:　　Hey, did you hear the news?

Mariko:　No, what happened?

Jeff:　　 I was awarded a scholarship .¹

Mariko:　 Wow, that's wonderful news .²

	1. 出来事	2. 反応
対話 ①	A Japanese scientist won a Nobel prize again	Wow. That's great news
対話 ②	I was asked to play on the soccer team	Well done. That's brilliant news
対話 ③	Florida was hit by a strong hurricane	Oh no. That's awful news

Let's check some more!

● 能動態から受動態に書き換える時は、be動詞が人称・数の点で主語と一致しているか、時制が同じかなどを確認してみましょう。

Reading : *Cherry Blossoms in Washington* 2-14

In 1912, about 3,000 cherry trees were sent to the United States by the Japanese people as a token of friendship. In a ceremony, the American First Lady and the wife of the Japanese ambassador planted the first two trees in West Potomac Park, Washington, D.C. A National Cherry Blossom Festival has been held in the park since 1935. In 1949, the first Cherry Blossom Queen was selected. In 1957, the Cherry Blossom Queen's crown with 1,585 pearls was donated by Mikimoto, a Japanese jewelry company. Currently, the National Cherry Blossom Festival is held for two weeks at the beginning of April every year.

A. 文中の受動態の部分に下線を引きましょう。

B. 質問文を読んで英語で答えましょう。

1. How many cherry trees were sent to the United States from Japan in 1912?

_____

2. Why were the trees sent to the United States?

_____

3. Where are the cherry blossoms seen?

_____

4. When was the first Cherry Blossom Queen chosen?

_____

5. How long does the festival in Washington, D.C. last?

_____

■ Writing

A. ある学生の「私の住む町」についての紹介文を読みましょう。 　(CD) 2-15

I live in Oume, Tokyo. Many events are held in my city every year. For example, there is a famous plum blossom festival in March. It is said that more than 300,000 people visit my city during the festival season. In summer, there is a fireworks festival in a big park on a hill. It is really fantastic. However, my favorite event is the Oume City Marathon in February. It started in 1967 and is known throughout the world. About 15,000 people from all over the world run the marathon, so the course is very crowded. All the runners are given T-shirts as a souvenir. I like running, so I want to take part in the marathon someday. I hope you have a chance to visit Oume in the future and see one of the events.

....

souvenir 記念品、土産

B. あなたの住んでいる町や故郷、あるいは学校の行事を書き出してみましょう。

Events	When / Where	Details (history, etc.)
(例) plum blossom festival	March	More than 300,000 visitors

C. 「私の住む町」(あるいは「私の故郷」、「私の大学」等) の行事について紹介文を書いてみましょう。

_____

_____

_____

_____

_____

_____

Amazing Animals 頻度を表す副詞

amazingとは「驚くべき」という意味です。このユニットでは、そんな驚くべき生態を持つ動物たちを題材に頻度の副詞（sometimesやalwaysなど）について学びましょう。

■ Vocabulary 英語の意味を下の日本語から選びましょう。 (CD) 2-16

1. sociable ( )   2. scared ( )   3. vegetarian ( )   4. poisonous ( )

5. classical music ( )   6. annually ( )   7. short-tempered ( )

8. shy ( )   9. talented ( )   10. friend for life ( )

a. クラシック音楽	b. 怖がった	c. 短気な	d. 菜食主義の	e. 才能のある
f. 社交的な	g. 恥ずかしがりの	h. 年一回	i. 有毒な	j. 生涯の友

■ Warm-up : Amazing Animal Quiz !!!

A. それぞれの絵の動物は英語で何というでしょうか。下のボックスから選んで写真の下に書きましょう。

1. _____ 2. _____ 3. _____ 4. _____ 5. _____

chimpanzee	dolphin	fox	polar bear	snake

B. ペアを組み、各動物についての記述が正しいと思ったらTrueに、誤りだと思ったらFalseに印をつけましょう。

	True	False
1. Dolphins often live for 30 to 40 years.	☐	☐
2. Dolphins are usually very sociable animals.	☐	☐
3. Snakes always hunt at night.	☐	☐
4. Snakes can sometimes eat children.	☐	☐
5. Polar bears never drink water.	☐	☐
6. Polar bears usually walk 15 miles a day.	☐	☐
7. When chimpanzees smile, they are usually scared.	☐	☐
8. Chimpanzees sometimes hunt and eat meat.	☐	☐
9. Foxes usually live alone.	☐	☐
10. Foxes never go to towns and cities.	☐	☐

CDを聞いて、答えをチェックしましょう。 (CD) 2-17

もう一度CDを聞き、下の( )を埋めて、答えを確認しましょう。 **repeat** 🔘 2-17

■ Dolphins ( ) ( ) very sociable animals and are friendly to humans. Moreover, they ( ) ( ) live for 30-40 years, so they might be ideal pets for us.

■ Snakes ( ) ( ) be dangerous. They hunt both during the day and at night. Although some big snakes ( ) ( ) eaten children, they ( ) ( ) smaller animals.

■ Polar bears are one of the few animals that ( ) ( ) water. They get all the water they need from their food. However, they have to walk very far to find food every day, sometimes as far as 15 miles.

■ Chimpanzees only smile when they are very scared. Many people think that chimpanzees are vegetarian, but when they are hungry, they ( ) ( ) and ( ) other animals for meat.

■ Foxes ( ) ( ) to towns and cities to look for food. However, you will probably only see one fox at one time. This is because foxes ( ) ( ) alone.

▓ **Grammar Point** : 頻度を表す副詞

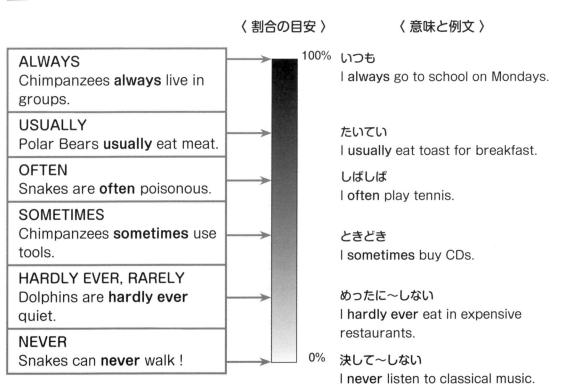

〈 割合の目安 〉　　　〈 意味と例文 〉

ALWAYS Chimpanzees **always** live in groups.	100%	いつも I always go to school on Mondays.
USUALLY Polar Bears **usually** eat meat.		たいてい I usually eat toast for breakfast.
OFTEN Snakes are **often** poisonous.		しばしば I often play tennis.
SOMETIMES Chimpanzees **sometimes** use tools.		ときどき I sometimes buy CDs.
HARDLY EVER, RARELY Dolphins are **hardly ever** quiet.		めったに～しない I hardly ever eat in expensive restaurants.
NEVER Snakes can **never** walk !	0%	決して～しない I never listen to classical music.

▶頻度を表す副詞の位置に注意しましょう！

一般動詞の前 (live, eat, goなど)	I **sometimes** go shopping
	私はときどき買い物に行く。
be動詞の後 (am, is, are, was, wereなど)	I am **always** late for class.
	私はいつも授業に遅れる。
助動詞の後 (can, may, mustなど)	I can **never** stay up all night.
	私は決して徹夜ができない。

■ Grammar Practice

A. (　　) 内の語句を並べ替えて、意味の通る英文にしましょう。

1. (usually, I, play, on Sundays, tennis).

   _____

2. (hardly ever, on weekends, he, studies).

   _____

3. (can, see, Mt. Fuji, I, in the winter, often).

   _____

4. (sometimes, tired, in the afternoon, I, am).

   _____

5. (on Mondays, gets up, always, she, early).

   _____

Let's check some more!

● 頻度を尋ねるには、"How often do you〜？" という聞き方を知っておくと便利です。
答えるときには、「いつも（always）」「ときどき（sometimes）」などの頻度を表す副詞のほかにも、「週に1、2回（once or twice a week）」や「3日ごと（every three days）」のような言い方もあります。

B. 選択肢の中で最も適切なものを選び、1〜5の英文を完成させましょう。

1. I am _____ very tired after working hard all day.

   (A) annually   (B) weekly   (C) usually   (D) on Sunday

2. Mary _____ her teeth before she goes to bed.

   (A) always brushes   (B) is always brushing

   (C) brushes always   (D) to always brush

3. He gets up very early _____.

   (A) always   (B) in the morning   (C) yesterday   (D) never

4. You _____ throw away your trash in the street.

   (A) never should   (B) never do   (C) should never   (D) to never

5. My professor _____ flies to New York. He went there ten times last year.

   (A) every day   (B) often   (C) never   (D) hardly ever

■ Dialogue

対話文を聞いた後、ペアで ☐ の部分を入れ替えて練習しましょう。最後は、☐ の部分を自分で考えて対話練習しましょう。 (CD) 2-18

Bill and Sarah are chatting after class.

Bill: What do you usually do after school?

Sarah: Well, I usually go straight home, but sometimes I go shopping .¹

Bill: What about on weekends ?²

Sarah: I always work because I have a part-time job .³

	1. 放課後の過ごし方	2. いつ	3. 時間の過ごし方
対話 ①	often have a coffee at Starbucks	on Sundays	usually volunteer at a pet rescue center
対話 ②	sometimes go to the gym	on Friday nights	always go out with friends
対話 ③	always practice judo with my club members	during the test period	often study in the library

Reading : *The Chinese Zodiac*

Rat 1960, 1972, 1984,1996, 2008, 2020 Rats are clever and are usually very successful.	**Ox** 1961, 1973, 1985, 1997, 2009, 2021 Ox people are usually quiet and friendly.	**Tiger** 1962, 1974, 1986, 1998, 2010 Tigers are usually kind but can sometimes be very short-tempered.
Rabbit 1963, 1975, 1987, 1999, 2011 Rabbits are lucky and are often good at business.	**Dragon** 1964, 1976, 1988, 2000, 2012 Dragons are sometimes quiet but kind.	**Snake** 1965, 1977, 1989, 2001, 2013 Snakes usually think deeply and are often kind to their friends.
Horse 1966, 1978, 1990, 2002, 2014 Horses are happy people but sometimes talk too much.	**Ram** 1967, 1979, 1991, 2003, 2015 Ram people are often good at art but are usually shy.	**Monkey** 1968, 1980, 1992, 2004, 2016 Monkeys are very clever and usually have good memories.
Rooster 1969, 1981, 1993, 2005, 2017 Roosters are very talented but sometimes only think about themselves.	**Dog** 1970, 1982, 1994, 2006, 2018 Dogs usually make good leaders but fight with friends.	**Pig** 1971, 1983, 1995, 2007, 2019 Pigs usually make friends for life and hate arguing.

A. 表中の頻度を表す副詞に○をつけましょう。

B. 1〜5の質問文を読んで英語で答えましょう。

1. What year were you born in?

_____

2. Which is your animal?

_____

3. What kind of personality does your animal have?

_____

4. Do you agree with the description? If not, which animal do you think best describes your personality?

_____

5. Which animal would make a good partner? And why?

_____

Writing

A. 以下のeメールを読みましょう。 2-19

> Dear friends,
> My name is Julie. Do you know about the Chinese Zodiac? My animal is the pig, so I love making friends. I study animal science at college. I go to school from Monday to Friday. I always get up early on Saturday mornings and go to the beach near the house with my friends. At the beach I enjoy surfing. After surfing I sometimes go to a restaurant for breakfast. I am usually tired at the end of the day but happy. On Sundays I hardly ever go to the beach. I usually stay at home, and I often surf the Internet to get a lot of amazing information about animals. I love animals, and I love the weekends! How do you usually spend your weekends?

B. あなた自身のいつもの週末の過ごし方を、左下のスケジュール表にメモしてみましょう。

C. 次に、スケジュール表をもとに、頻度を表す副詞をできるだけ使ってJulieにあなたの週末の過ごし方について英語で手紙を書きましょう。

Saturday

Sunday

Dear Julie,
_____
_____
_____
_____
_____
_____
_____
_____
_____
_____
_____

Feelings -ing, -edで終わる形容詞

このユニットでは、自分の感情を表す表現を学びながら、-ingで終わる形容詞と-edで終わる形容詞の違いを理解し、使い分けができるようにしましょう。

■ Vocabulary 英語の意味を下の日本語から選びましょう。 🎧 2-20

1. embarrassed (　)　　2. bored (　)　　3. annoyed (　)

4. inside out (　)　　5. disappointed (　)　　6. to affect (　)

7. to reduce (　)　　8. stress (　)　　9. to achieve (　)

10. benefit (　)

a. がっかりした	b. 影響を及ぼす	c. 利点	d. 裏返しに	e. 減らす
f. 退屈した	g. 精神的重圧	h. 当惑した	i. いらいらした	j. 成し遂げる

■ Warm-up : How Do You Feel?

絵を見て、それぞれの人の感情を表すのにぴったりの形容詞を見つけましょう。

□にアルファベットを書きましょう。

a. embarrassed	b. excited	c. bored	d. annoyed	e. surprised

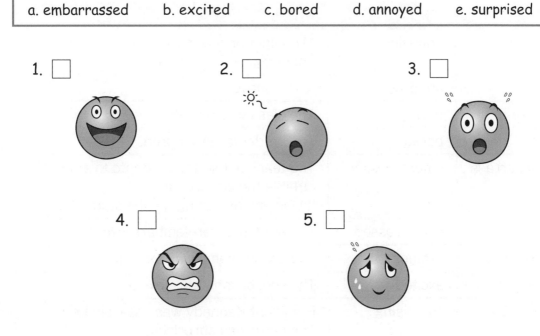

1. □   2. □   3. □

4. □   5. □

 CDを聞いて、答えをチェックしましょう。 🎧 2-21

もう一度 CD を聞き、下の（　）を埋めて、答えを確認しましょう。 repeat 2-21

1. I am going to watch a soccer game. I am really (　　　　　　　　)!

2. I have nothing to do today. I am very (　　　　　　　).

3. I saw a snake in my locker. I was very (　　　　　　　)!

4. My neighbor never stops talking about herself. I always get (　　　　　　　)
   when I am with her.

5. Yesterday I wore my shirt inside out. I was very (　　　　　　　).

■ Grammar Point : -ing, -ed で終わる形容詞

▶ 人の感情に影響を与えるような他動詞に -ing や -ed がつくと、多くの場合形容詞となります。語尾が、-ing なのか -ed なのかで意味が違ってきます。

The lesson **interested** me.（その授業は私に興味を持たせた。）

　= The lesson was **interesting** and I was **interested**.
　（その授業は面白くて、私は興味を持った。）

Tom **bored** me.（トムは私を退屈させた。）

　= Tom was **boring** and I was **bored**.（トムは退屈な人で、私は退屈した。）

動　詞	形容詞	例　文
annoy	annoying	My neighbor never stops talking. She is annoying.
	annoyed	I am annoyed.
bore	boring	The class was boring.
	bored	The students were bored.
embarrass	embarrassing	The teacher told the students to stand outside the classroom. It was embarrassing for the students.
	embarrassed	The students were embarrassed.
excite	exciting	The soccer game was exciting.
	excited	The soccer fans were excited.
surprise	surprising	President Kennedy was assassinated. The news was surprising.
	surprised	Everybody was surprised.

▶ -ing , -ed で終わる感情を表す形容詞には通例以下の特徴があります。

	例 文
very で修飾できる	He was very surprised.
比較変化する	I felt more tired.
名詞の前にきて名詞を修飾する	There was surprising news.
補語になる	He looked tired.

█ Grammar Practice

A. （ ）内の語を適切な形にして、下線部に書きましょう。

1. The lesson was _____. (interest)

2. I was _____ in the lesson. (interest)

3. The party was _____. (bore)

4. Tom is really _____ because his proposal was finally accepted. (thrill)

5. Mary got engaged, so she is very _____. (excite)

B. 選択肢の中で最も適切なものを選び、1～5の英文を完成させましょう.

1. It is _____ that you have won the first prize.
   (A) amazement　　(B) amazing　　　(C) amaze　　　(D) amazed

2. If you are _____ about anything, contact me.
   (A) confusing　　(B) confuse　　　(C) confused　　(D) to confuse

3. My girlfriend was so _____ that I broke up with her.
   (A) bore　　　　(B) boredom　　　(C) boring　　　(D) bored

4. You do not have to _____ everyone.
   (A) pleasing　　(B) pleased　　　(C) please　　　(D) be pleased

5. When President Kennedy was assassinated, the news _____ everyone around the world.
   (A) shocking　　(B) have shocked　(C) shock　　　　(D) shocked

◼ Dialogue

CDを聞いて、対話文の（　）を埋めましょう。ペアで対話練習をしましょう。　🄒 2-22

Carol and Tony are talking about their friend Bill.

Carol: I haven't seen Bill for a long time. How is he doing?

Tony: He's not so (　　　　　　).

Carol: Why is that?

Tony: He's very (　　　　　　) that he failed the test.

Carol: How about cheering him up?

Tony: What should we do?

Carol: Let's go bungee jumping together. It's very (　　　　　　).

Tony: No way! It's really (　　　　　　).

Let's check some more!

● このユニットで扱った「-ing, -ed で終わる感情を表す形容詞」は、動詞の現在分詞や過去分詞が完全に形容詞化したもので、形容詞と同じような特徴があります。一方、形容詞的に用いる動詞の現在分詞（-ing）と過去分詞（-ed）の用法は、完全に形容詞化したものとは多少違います。

Reading : *Yoga*  2-23

Are you interested in doing yoga? Yoga was developed thousands of years ago as a spiritual practice in India. However, today, most people do yoga because they find it relaxing, or it reduces their stress from their tiring daily lives. The word "yoga" comes from the Sanskrit word for union because practicing it is said to connect the body, breath, and mind. In order to achieve this union, yoga uses physical postures, breathing exercises, and meditation. Yoga's health benefits include lowering your blood pressure and heart rate and improving your self-confidence. That's why many people feel refreshed and much healthier after doing yoga. There are now many types of yoga such as hot yoga. This is when you do yoga in a hot room, between 35 and 40 degrees Centigrade. Now most cities in Japan have yoga classes, so it is easy to try it and discover how good it makes you feel.

....

spiritual practice 行（仏教）　**Sanskrit** 梵語（ぼんご）（古代インドの文語）
union 融和、和合　**posture** 姿勢　**meditation** 瞑想　**blood pressure** 血圧
heart rate 心拍数　**self-confidence** 自信

A. 文中から感情を表す形容詞を見つけて下線を引きましょう。

B. 質問文を読んで英語で答えましょう。

1. Where was yoga first developed?

   _____

2. Which language is the word "yoga" from?

   _____

3. What is yoga said to connect?

   _____

4. Why do many people feel refreshed and healthier after doing yoga?

   _____

5. What is "hot yoga"?

   _____

Writing

A. 以下の英作文を読んで、書いてある内容を表（Table 1)にまとめてみましょう。

An Unforgettable Trip

Last year I went to California on a home stay. I had a great time, but three memories will stay with me forever. The first was a trip to Los Angeles. I saw lots of gorgeous mansions in Beverly Hills. I was especially excited because I saw a movie star on a street. Second, I went to Sea World in San Diego and fed a dolphin. It was an amazing experience. Best of all, I went to Las Vegas and won a thousand dollars at a casino. I was so surprised and thrilled. It was a trip I will never forget.

Table 1		
Topics	How was it?	How did Ken feel?
movie star		excited
dolphin	amazing	
casino		surprised and thrilled

B. 次に、表（Table 1）を参考にして、あなたにとって印象に残った3つのできごとについて表（Table 2）に記入しましょう。

Table 2		
Topics	How was it?	How did you feel?

C. 表（Table 2）をもとに、あなたにとって印象に残った3つのできごとについて書きましょう。

_____

_____

_____

_____

_____

_____

World Quiz 原級、比較級、最上級

「世界で一番大きい○○は？」というようなクイズの答えは時と共に変わることもあります。
このユニットでは、世界の地理や文化を題材に、英語の比較表現について学びましょう。

■ Vocabulary 英語の意味を下の日本語から選びましょう。 🔘 2-25

1. world heritage (　)　　　2. site (　)　　　　　3. attractive (　)
4. no longer (　)　　5. to produce (　)　　6. view (　)　　7. distance (　)
8. destruction (　)　　　　9. gallery (　)　　　10. to run (　)

| a. 破壊　　　b. 世界遺産　　　c. 画廊　　　d. 眺め　　　e. 魅力的な　　　f. 場所 |
| g.（劇・映画などの上演が）続く　　h. 遠い地点、距離　　i. もはや〜でない　　j. 生産する |

■ Warm-up : Trivia Quiz

クイズを読んで正解と思うものに○をしましょう。

1. Which country is larger, Russia or Canada?
   a. Russia　　　　　　　　b. Canada

2. Which country has a larger population?
   a. Japan　　　　　　　　b. Australia

3. Which tower is higher, the Eiffel Tower or Tokyo Tower?
   a. Eiffel Tower　　　　　b. Tokyo Tower

4. Which is more popular in the United States, American football or soccer?
   a. American football　　　b. soccer

5. Where is the tallest building in the world?
   a. in the U.S.　　　　　b. in Taiwan　　　　　c. in Dubai

CDを聞いて、答えをチェックしましょう。 🔘 2-26

もう一度CDを聞き、下の ( ) を埋めて、答えを確認しましょう。 repeat 🔘2-26

1. Russia is ( ) ( ) Canada. Russia is ( ) ( )
   country in the world.
2. Japan has a much ( ) population, but the land of Japan is half
   ( ) ( ) ( ) that of Australia.
3. Tokyo Tower is ( ) than the Eiffel Tower by 13 meters.
4. American football is ( ) ( ) ( ) soccer in the
   United States. American football is ( ) ( ) ( )
   sport in the United States.
5. ( ) ( ) building in the world is in Dubai.
   ( ) ( ) ( ) is in Shanghai.

▚ Grammar Point：原級、比較級、最上級

▶ 「同じ」なのか「他方より～」なのか「一番～」なのかを表現するには、それぞれ原級、
比較級、最上級を使います。

▶ 原級は＜as＋(形容詞・副詞の原級)＋as＞の形をとります。比較級・最上級を作るには、一
般的に、短い単語は語尾に-er, -estをつけ、長い単語は語の前にmore, mostをつけます。

＊短い単語とは1音節またはy, er, ow, leで終わる2音節の単語のことを指し、長い単語とは、大部分の
2音節以上（yで終わる単語を除く）の単語を指します。

原級 **as** (形容詞/副詞) **as...** …と同じくらい～ **as many** (名詞) **as...** **as much** (名詞) **as...** …と同じ数/量の～	Japan is almost as large as California. 日本はカリフォルニアとほぼ同じ大きさだ。
	China has as many world heritage sites as Italy does. 中国にはイタリアと同じ数の世界遺産がある。
比較級 (形容詞/副詞) **er than...** **more** (形容詞/副詞) **than** ... …よりも～だ	Alaska is larger than Texas. アラスカはテキサスより大きい。
	Tokyo prices are more expensive than Seoul prices. 東京はソウルよりも物価が高い。
最上級 **the** (形容詞/副詞) **est** **the most** (形容詞/副詞) 一番～だ	Burj Khalifa is the tallest building in the world. ブルジュ・ハリファは世界で一番高いビルだ。
	I think Tokyo is the most attractive city in the world. 東京は世界で一番魅力的な町だと思う。

■ Grammar Practice

A. (　　) 内の語句を並べ替えて、意味の通る英文にしましょう。

1. (large, is, Alaska, Japan, as, as, not).

   _____

2. (or, is, longer, which, the Mississippi, the Nile)?

   _____

3. (country, is, smallest, the Vatican City, the world, in, the).

   _____

4. Mt. Fuji (is, famous, the, Japan, mountain, in, most).

   _____

5. (the world, the, what, is, island, in, largest)?

   _____

B. 選択肢の中で最も適切なものを選び、1～5の英文を完成させましょう。

1. Korea is not as large _____ Japan.
   (A) to   (B) as   (C) than   (D) so

2. Greenland is the _____ island in the world.
   (A) large   (B) larger   (C) largest   (D) enlarge

3. London is a _____ city than New York.
   (A) expensive (B) more expensive (C) most expensive (D) too expensive

4. The Nile is _____ longer than the Mississippi.
   (A) very   (B) more   (C) much   (D) too

5. China produces the _____ potatoes in the world.
   (A) many   (B) much   (C) more   (D) most

◼ Dialogue

対話文を聞いた後、ペアで ☐ の部分を入れ替えて練習しましょう。最後は、☐ の部分を自分で考えて対話練習しましょう。 ⊙CD 2-27

Lillian is answering Ken's questions at a school quiz night.

Ken: Who is richer, Bill Gates or the Sultan of Brunei ?[1]

Lillian: I think Bill Gates is richer. He is one of the richest people in the world .[2]

Ken: That's right, well done. . . OK next question. . .

	1. 比較の質問	2. 答え
対話 ①	Which city is more expensive, Tokyo or Madrid	Tokyo is more expensive than Madrid. It is one of the most expensive cities in the world
対話 ②	Which mountain is higher, Mount Fuji or Mont Blanc	Mont Blanc is higher. It is one of the highest mountains in Europe
対話 ③	Which city has a larger population, Tokyo or Beijing	Beijing has a larger population than Tokyo

Let's check some more!

● 比較級や最上級を強めるときは、much や (by) far などを使います。
   (例) Mt. Everest is much higher than Mt. Fuji.
   (例) Mt. Everest is by far the highest mountain in the world.
● 倍数は次のように表します。
   (例) Japan is half as large as Australia.
   (例) The population of the U.S. is twice as large as that of Japan.

Reading : *New York City* 2-28

 New York is one of the biggest cities in the world and one of the most popular tourist spots. The view of Manhattan seen from a distance is really beautiful. The Empire State Building was the tallest building in the world from 1931 until 1972. After the destruction of the World Trade Center in 2001, it became the tallest building again. However, the new World Trade Center was constructed in 2012, and now the Empire State Building is the third tallest building in Manhattan.

You can also enjoy wonderful art in New York. The Metropolitan Museum is one of the largest art museums in the world, and there are many other smaller museums or galleries. Moreover, New York has other special art events: dance, theater, music, and musicals. Popular musicals usually run for a very long time. The longest running musical on Broadway is *The Phantom of the Opera*. It started in 1988 and is still running now.

....

Manhattan マンハッタン（ニューヨーク市の中枢をなす島）　**theater** 演劇
to run 続演される

A. 文中の比較級、最上級の部分に下線を引きましょう。

B. 次の文が英文の内容と合っていればT、合っていなければFと書きましょう。

1. New York is very big but not so popular with tourists. 　　(　)

2. The Empire State Building is no longer the tallest building in Manhattan.
　　　　　　　　　　　　　　　　　　　　　　　　　　　　　　(　)

3. The Empire State Building was not as tall as the old World Trade Center.
　　　　　　　　　　　　　　　　　　　　　　　　　　　　　　(　)

4. The Metropolitan Museum is one of the smaller galleries. 　　(　)

5. *The Phantom of the Opera* is a musical that has run longer than any other musical. 　　(　)

Writing

次の資料を見て、南北アメリカの五カ国を比較する文を7つ作りましょう。

（例）There are more people in Argentina than. . .

　　　Argentina is larger than. . .

　　　Paraguay produces more soybeans than. . .

　　　_____ produces the most soybeans of the five countries.

　　　_____ has the most world heritage sites of the five countries.

	U.S.A.	Brazil	Paraguay	Bolivia	Argentina
Population (million)	328	277	7	11	41
Area (ha)	963	852	41	110	278
Production of soybeans (1,000t)	106,934	100,000	8,800	3,100	59,000
Number of world heritage sites	24	22	1	7	11

1. _____

2. _____

3. _____

4. _____

5. _____

6. _____

7. _____

Business 基本的な前置詞

時間や場所を表すのに欠かせない語が前置詞です。「×時に」「△月△日に」「○○年に」、あるいは「×駅で」「△通りで」「○○市で」などの「に」や「で」にあたります。ビジネスを題材に、基本的な前置詞の使い方を身につけましょう。

■ Vocabulary 英語の意味を下の日本語から選びましょう。 (CD) 2-29

1. to establish (　)　　2. factory (　)　　　　3. headquarters (　)
4. manager (　)　　　5. entertainment industry (　)　　6. to enroll (　)
7. to co-found (　)　　8. to introduce (　)　　9. to be fired (　)　　10. CEO (　)

a. 支配人、部長　　b. 設立する　　c. 導入する　　d. 解雇される　　e. 共同で設立する	
f. 娯楽産業　　g. 最高経営責任者　　h. 工場　　i. 入会する、入学する　　j. 本社、本部	

■ Warm-up : From Small Company to Big Business

次の6つの会社の創始者、創立時期、創立場所を下のボックスから選び、アルファベットをリストの下線に書きましょう。

	Company	Founder's name	Time (year)	Place
①	HONDA The Power of Dreams	Soichiro Honda	_____	_____
②	Häagen-Dazs	_____		The Bronx, New York
③	Kellogg's	Will Kellogg	_____	_____
④	adidas	_____	1924	_____
⑤	Panasonic	_____	_____	Osaka
⑥	Apple Inc.	_____	1976	_____

CDを聞いて答えを余白に書き入れ、選んだアルファベットが合っていたか確認しましょう。 (CD) 2-30

Name	a. Konosuke Matsushita　　b. Steve Jobs c. Reuben and Rose Mattus　　d. Adolf Dassler
Time	e. 1906　　f. 1918　　g. 1948　　h. 1961
Place	i. a small village near Nuremberg, Germany　　j. Cupertino, California k. Hamamatsu, Shizuoka　　l. Battle Creek, Michigan

もう一度 CD を聞き、下の（　）を埋めて、答えを確認しましょう。　repeat　CD 2-30

1. (　　　　　　　) September 24, 1948, Soichiro Honda established the Honda Motor Co. (　　　　　　　) Hamamatsu, Shizuoka.

2. Haagen-Dazs was established by Reuben and Rose Mattus (　　　　　　) the Bronx in New York (　　　　　　) 1961.

3. (　　　　　　) 1906, (　　　　　　) the age of 45, Will Kellogg opened his own breakfast cereal company (　　　　　　) Battle Creek, Michigan. It was renamed the Kellogg Company (　　　　　　) 1922.

4. Adidas was started by two brothers named Adi and Rudolf Dassler (　　　　　　) 1924 (　　　　　　) a small village near Nuremberg, Germany.

5. (　　　　　　) the age of 23, Konosuke Matsushita founded the Matsushita Electric Appliance Factory (　　　　　) Osaka (　　　　　) 1918. It was renamed twice and became Panasonic (　　　　　) 2008.

6. (　　　　　　) April 1, 1976, Steve Jobs co-founded Apple Computer Inc. in the Jobs' family garage (　　　　　　) Cupertino, California. He was still (　　　　　) his early 20's.

■ Grammar Point：基本的な前置詞（at, on, in）

▶場所

at	↓ （的）の一点に	Someone is standing at the door.（場所としての点） Students study at school.（場所としての点） I arrived at Tokyo Station.（到達点）
on	↓ （線・面上）に接して	There is a message on the table.（テーブルの上に） They sell toys on the 7th floor.（7階で） The shop is on Fifth Avenue.（5番街に面して）
in	↗↘ （区域・空間）の中に	They started the company in a small village. The file is in the cabinet. His office is in the Mori Tower.

▶時

at	特定の時	They close the office at 5:30. （時刻） At the age of 40, he opened his shop. （年齢）
on	特定の日	Steve Jobs was born on February 24, 1955. （日付） We have a meeting on Friday. （曜日） We meet on Friday afternoon. （特定の日の午前／午後／夕方）
in	特定の期間 （月、季節、年、 年代、世紀など）	He called me in the evening. （午前／午後／夕方） The course ends sometime in July. （月） We opened a new shop in (the) spring. （季節） It was renamed the Kellogg Company in 1922.（年）

▮ Grammar Practice

A. （　）内の語を並べ替えて、意味の通る英文にしましょう。

1. (at, closes, office, 5 p.m., the).

_____

2. (I, on, don't, Sundays, work).

_____

3. (company, founded, 1950, my, was, in).

_____

4. (opening, factory, in, are, a, Vietnam, we).

_____

5. (the, can, entrance, we, at, meet)?

_____

B. 選択肢の中で最も適切なものを選び、1～5の英文を完成させましょう。

1. I haven't seen Bill _____ a few days. I last saw him on Monday.
   (A) on   (B) for   (C) since   (D) in

2. The headquarters of the company are _____ a small town in southern Germany.

(A) at   (B) of   (C) in   (D) on

3. Mr. Smith has lived in Germany _____ 2005.

(A) for   (B) since   (C) on   (D) in

4. I read about the new product _____ a newspaper.

(A) on   (B) at   (C) in   (D) by

5. Our manager will call you _____ a few days.

(A) by   (B) on   (C) in   (D) at

▌Dialogue

対話文の（　　　）に適当な前置詞を入れましょう。CDを聞いて答えを確認し、ペアで対話練習をしましょう。 🎧 2-31

Two businesspeople are talking on the phone.

Man: I called your home (   ) about 9 o'clock last night, but you were not there.

Woman: I was (   ) Kyoto. I took the last Shinkansen and arrived (   ) Tokyo Station at just around midnight. Why did you call?

Man: Well, our company is holding a party (   ) the Shibuya Hotel (   ) Friday. Can you come?

Woman: I think I can, but I have a meeting (   ) the afternoon. What time does it start?

Man: (   ) 5:00 p.m. . . .

Let's check some more!

- 時を表す in は、月、季節、年など時間的に幅のある期間で使われるほか、「今から〜後に」あるいは「〜かかって」の意味でもよく使われます。

   （例）I'll call you again in a few days.（2〜3日したらまた電話します。）

   （例）He will be back home in 10 minutes.（彼は10分で帰宅するだろう。）

   （例）I learned German in three years.（私は3年でドイツ語を身につけた。）

Steve Jobs was probably the most powerful businessman (① 　　) both the computer and entertainment industries. Jobs was born (② 　　) February 24, 1955 (③ 　　) San Francisco, California. Soon after birth, he was put up for adoption. (④ 　　) 1972, he enrolled (⑤ 　　) Reed College in Portland, Oregon, but soon dropped out. (⑥ 　　) the autumn of 1974, Jobs returned to California and took a job at a video game company. (⑦ 　　) 21, he co-founded Apple Computer Co. and introduced its first personal computers, the Apple I and II. (⑧ 　　) 1984, the company produced its most famous product, the Macintosh. Although it was very successful, he was suddenly fired from Apple (⑨ 　　) the age of 30. Soon he founded another computer company, NeXT and started an animation company, Pixar. When Apple Inc. bought NeXT in 1997, Jobs returned to the company to serve as its CEO. After that, Apple continued to roll out revolutionary products, such as the iPod, iPhone, and iPad. Steve Jobs died (⑩ 　　) October 5, 2011.

....

was put up for adoption 養子に出された　**roll out**（新製品を）売り出す

A. 文中の（　）に適当な前置詞を入れて、文章を完成させましょう。

B. 次の文が英文の内容と合っていればT、合っていなければFと書きましょう。

1. Steve Jobs was the most powerful businessman in the entertainment industry.　　　　　　　　　　　　　　　　　　　　　　(　)

2. He graduated from Reed College in Oregon.　　　　　　　(　)

3. He founded his first company in 1976.　　　　　　　　　(　)

4. He was fired from Apple because the Macintosh was not successful.　(　)

5. After he returned to Apple, he became its CEO.　　　　　(　)

 **Writing**

ホンダ技研工業の創始者、本田宗一郎氏の略年表です。この表をもとに、必要な情報を選び、適当な前置詞を使って本田宗一郎氏を紹介する文章を書いてみましょう。（単調な文章にならないように、ReadingのSteve Jobs紹介文を参考にしましょう。）

When	(Age)	Where	What
17/11/1906		Hamamatsu, Shizuoka	was born
1922	(16)	Hamamatsu Tokyo	• graduated from Futamata Senior Elementary School • started working at an auto repair shop called Art Shokai
1928	(22)	Hamamatsu	• returned from Tokyo • opened his own repair shop
1936	(30)	Hamamatsu	• built and raced his own racing car • was seriously injured in a car race
24/9/1948	(42)	Hamamatsu	founded Honda Motor Co. to produce motorcycles
1953	(47)	(Tokyo)	moved the headquarters to Tokyo
by 1955	(49)	(Japan)	Honda became the leading motorcycle manufacturer
1959	(53)	Los Angeles, U.S.A.	established the first store abroad
1962	(56)		started producing cars
by 1963	(57)	(U.S.A.)	Honda became the top-selling motorcycle company
1965	(59)	Mexico	Honda racing team first won the F1 Grand Prix
1973	(67)		retired
5/8/1991	(84)	Tokyo	died

_____

_____

_____

_____

_____

_____

_____

_____

Unit 19

Environment 接続詞 (2)

異常気象や絶滅危惧種の増大など、地球温暖化の問題は近年益々深刻化しています。このユニットでは環境問題を題材に、when, because, although, if などの従位接続詞について学びましょう。

■Vocabulary 英語の意味を下の日本語から選びましょう。 (CD) 2-33

1. endangered (　) 　　2. hunger (　) 　　3. land development (　)

4. to protect (　) 　　5. global warming (　) 　　6. to melt (　)

7. to disappear (　) 　　8. to release (　) 　　9. impact (　)

10. climate (　)

a. 排出する	b. 土地開発	c. 溶ける	d. 飢え	e. 守る
f. 地球温暖化	g. 気候	h. 消える	i. 影響	j. 絶滅のおそれがある

■Warm-up : Endangered Animals

下は絶滅のおそれがある動物たちです。CDを聞いて、それぞれの動物の説明としてあてはまる番号を□の中に入れましょう。下線には、その動物が住む地域を書きましょう。 (CD) 2-34

A. □

B. □

＿＿＿＿＿＿＿＿＿＿＿　　　＿＿＿＿＿＿＿＿＿＿＿

C. □

D. □

＿＿＿＿＿＿＿＿＿＿＿　　　＿＿＿＿＿＿＿＿＿＿＿

109

もう一度CDを聞き、下の (　　) を埋めて、答えを確認しましょう。　(repeat)　(CD) 2-34

1. They are the largest animals in the world, and they live in all oceans.
    (　　　　　　　　) they were heavily hunted during the 20th century, some kinds
    of them are highly endangered.

2. They live only in the mountains of China. Many of them died of hunger
    (　　　　　　　　　) humans destroyed many bamboo forests for land
    development. They were also hunted. (　　　　　　) there are over 50
    protected areas today, they are still endangered.

3. They live on sea ice near the North Pole. (　　　　　　) we don't stop global
    warming, the sea ice will keep melting and they will lose places to hunt food.
    Most of them will disappear from the earth within 50 years.

4. They are the largest member of the cat family. Their main home today is
    India. They lived in China before, but people hated them. (　　　　　　)
    people found them, they were killed. Now no one has seen the animal in
    China for more than 25 years.

▌Grammar Point：従位接続詞 (when, because, although, if)

▶主節と従節を結びつけるのが（従位）接続詞です。時や理由、譲歩、条件などの副詞節を
導くのによく使う接続詞は以下の通りです。

when …のとき (時を表す)	You should bring your own bag when you go shopping. (⇒When you go shopping, you should bring your own bag.)
	買物に行くときには自分のバッグを持参するべきだ。
because …なので (理由を表す)	The rainforest is getting smaller because people cut down or burn trees. (⇒Because people cut down or burn trees, the rainforest is getting smaller.)
	人々が木を伐採したり焼いたりするので、熱帯雨林が小さくなっている。
although …だけれども (譲歩を表す)	Although global warming is a difficult problem, there should be something we can do. (⇒There should be something we can do although global warming is a difficult problem.)
	地球温暖化は難しい問題だが、何か私たちにできることがあるはずだ。

if …ならば （条件を表す）	If the earth gets warmer at this speed, some islands will be under water soon. (⇒Some islands will be under water soon if the earth gets warmer at this speed.) ・・・ この速度で地球温暖化が進めば、じきにいくつかの島が水中に沈んでしまうだろう。

Grammar Practice

A. （　　）の中の接続詞を、それぞれの文の適当な所に入れて英文を完成させましょう。必要に応じてカンマも入れましょう。

1. the earth is getting warmer there is more CO_2 in the air.（because）

   _____

2. people use oil as energy CO_2 is released.（when）

   _____

3. sea ice is disappearing the earth is getting warmer.（because）

   _____

4. more and more sea ice melts many people and animals will lose their living places.（if）

   _____

5. people try to protect endangered animals some will disappear from the earth in the future.（although）

   _____

B. 選択肢の中で最も適切なものを選び、1～5の英文を完成させましょう。

1. _____ we use less oil, coal, or gas, the CO_2 level will go down.
   (A) But　　　　　(B) If　　　　　(C) Although　　　　(D) Because

2. _____ driving to work is convenient, it uses more energy than taking a train.
   (A) When　　　　(B) Although　　　(C) But　　　　　(D) If

3. More and more sea ice melts _____ the earth gets warmer.
   (A) although   (B) but   (C) so   (D) when

4. _____ a lot of sea ice melts, the sea level will get higher.
   (A) If   (B) Although   (C) So   (D) But

5. The air around the highway is dirty _____ there are so many cars.
   (A) but   (B) although   (C) because   (D) so

■ Dialogue

( ) に when, because, although, if のいずれかを入れましょう。CDを聞いて答えを確認し、ペアで対話練習をしましょう。 🎧 2-35

Ken and Julie are talking about pandas.

Ken: What animals did you see (   ) you went to the zoo?

Julie: Pandas, elephants, lions, monkeys. . . But not many kinds (   )
we didn't have much time.

Ken: Did you know the giant panda is endangered?

Julie: Yes, I did. There were only 1,800 pandas left in the wild. Now pandas are
protected by law. (   ) they are not protected, they will
disappear from the earth.

Ken: Pandas eat bamboo (   ) they are a member of the meat-eating
bear family. Isn't that interesting?

Let's check some more!

● but と although [though] の用法の違いに注意しましょう。
   (例) Although hunting elephants is prohibited, some people still hunt them.
   (例) Hunting pandas is prohibited, but some people still hunt them.
● 従位接続詞に導かれる節は従節と呼ばれますが、必ず主節とともに用いられ、単独で使
   われることはありません。
   (例) × Because the earth is getting warmer.
      ○ Sea ice is disappearing because the earth is getting warmer.
● when, because, although, if などで導かれる副詞節の位置の入れ替えは可能です。
   主文が文頭のときは従文との間にカンマは不要です。
   (例) When people burn oil, coal, or gas, CO_2 is released.
      ⇒ CO_2 is released when people burn oil, coal, or gas.

Reading : *The Loss of the Amazon Forest* 2-36

The Amazon rainforest is under attack. More and more trees are burned or cut down every year. People cut down the trees of the forest (① although / because) they want space to keep cows. People also burn the forest (② if / because) the ash of trees makes the soil rich to grow vegetables. About 20 percent of the Amazon rainforest has been lost in the past 40 years. (③ If / Although) the rainforest continues to be destroyed at this speed, many kinds of living things in the Amazon rainforest will become endangered. The loss of the rainforest has an impact on the climate. It gets warmer and it rains less in Brazil. (④ Although / Because) the Brazilian government is trying to protect the rainforest by looking out for illegal cutting, they cannot stop it completely.

....

rainforest 熱帯雨林　**burn** 燃やす　**ash** 灰　**soil** 土壌　**grow** 育てる　**illegal** 違法の

A. 文中の（　）の中から適語を選びましょう。

B. 次の文が英文の内容と合っていればT、合っていなければFと書きましょう。

1. People burn the rainforest to get better soil. 　　　　　　　　　（　　）

2. People cut down trees to sell the land. 　　　　　　　　　　　　（　　）

3. About half of living things have been lost in the Amazon rainforest. 　（　　）

4. The climate of Brazil has changed because of the destruction of the rainforest. 　　　　　　　　　　　　　　　　　　　　　　　（　　）

5. The government does not do anything to protect the rainforest. 　（　　）

Writing

A. 以下はマリが地球温暖化防止のために行っていることのリストです。 2-37

What I do to help slow down global warming

- I bring my own cloth bag <u>when</u> I go to a supermarket.
- I turn off the water <u>while</u> I am brushing my teeth.
- In winter, I wear a lot of clothing and set the room temperature lower <u>although</u> it is not so comfortable.
- <u>When</u> I finish drinking something in a PET bottle, I bring the empty bottle to a recycling bin at a convenience store.
- I don't take *waribashi* (disposable wooden chopsticks) <u>when</u> I buy a lunch box at a convenience store.

B. あなたが地球温暖化防止のために行っていること、またはできることのリストを下に作りましょう。その際に when, because, although, if などの従位接続詞をできるだけ使ってみましょう。

_____

_____

_____

_____

_____

_____

_____

_____

_____

_____

_____

_____

_____

_____

_____

Old Sayings 不定詞と動名詞

心に残る名言というものがあります。このユニットでは、いわゆることわざ（old saying）を使いながら不定詞と動名詞について学びましょう。

▰ Vocabulary　英語の意味を下の日本語から選びましょう。　(CD) 2-38

1. stuff (　　)　　　　2. to postpone (　　)　　　3. to be frank with you (　　)
4. to celebrate (　　)　　5. to hesitate (　　)　　6. to contact (　　)
7. can't afford to (　　)　8. to be based on (　　)　9. to attempt (　　)
10. remedy (　　)

a. 祝う	b. 試みる	c. ～する余裕がない	d. 率直にいうと	e. ためらう
f. 延期する	g. 治療法	h. ～に基づいている	i. もの	j. 連絡する

▰ Warm-up : Let's Play *Karuta*!

CDを聞き、カルタの内容を説明している英文の番号を□に入れましょう。　(CD) 2-39

A. □

わらうかど
には
ふくきたる

B. □

やすもの
かひの
ぜにうしなひ

C. □

いっすん
さきは
やみ

D. □

おに
に
かなぼう

E. □

いぬも
あるけば
ぼうにあたる

F. □

うそから
でた
まこと

もう一度CDを聞き、下の（　）を埋めて、答えを確認しましょう。　**repeat** 🎧 2-39

1. (　　　　　　　) cheap stuff is (　　　　　　　) money.

2. A strong man becomes stronger by (　　　　　　) an iron club.

3. You should expect anything (　　　　　) (　　　　　) in the future.

4. (　　　　　) will make you happy.

5. You sometimes find the truth by (　　　　) a lie.

6. A walking dog will always find something (　　　　　) (　　　　　).

▮ **Grammar Point**：不定詞と動名詞

▶ ＜to＋動詞の原形＞の形の不定詞や、＜動詞＋ing＞の形の動名詞の主な用法は以下の通りです。

形	文中での働き	例文
不定詞 (to V) （名詞的用法）	主語	To be or not to be, that is the question. 生きるべきか死すべきか、それが問題だ。
	目的語	If you hope to be an actor, you need to practice acting. 役者になりたいなら演技の練習をする必要がある。
	補語	The most important thing in life is to learn how to give love. 人生で一番大事なことは愛をいかに与えるかを知ることである。
不定詞 (to V) （形容詞的用法）	名詞を修飾	There is nothing to eat in the house. 家には食べるものはない。
不定詞 (to V) （副詞的用法）	文全体を 修飾	To be frank with you, I don't like the way you behave. 率直にいうと、あなたのふるまいが気に入らない。
	目的を表す	We go to school (in order/so as) to study. 勉強するために学校に通う。
	原因、理由	I'm glad to meet you. お目にかかれて嬉しい。
	結果	She went to America, never to return to Japan. 彼女はアメリカに渡り、日本には戻ってこなかった。

形	文中での働き	例 文
動名詞 (V ing) 名詞扱い	主語、補語	Seeing is believing. 百聞は一見にしかず。
	目的語	Do not postpone doing what you can do today. 今日できることは明日にのばすな。
	前置詞の 目的語	It goes without saying that life is full of wonders. 人生は驚きで満ちていることはいうまでもない。

Grammar Practice

A. (　　) 内の語を並べ替えて、意味の通る英文にしましょう。

1. If you are a college student, it is important to (time, get, class, on, to).

   _____

2. I am thirsty. Would you please give (something, me, drink, to, cold)?

   _____

3. Tom went to a convenience store (buy, a, to, order, in) newspaper.

   _____

4. Tom was asked by his father (to, stay, not, late, up).

   _____

5. My grandmother lived (90th, celebrate, her, birthday, to).

   _____

B. 選択肢の中で最も適切なものを選び、1〜5の英文を完成させましょう.

1. Ann wants _____ by everybody.

   (A) to like   (B) liking   (C) to be liked   (D) being liked

2. I am looking forward to _____ you soon.

   (A) see   (B) seeing   (C) having seen   (D) be seeing

3. What do you say _____ out tonight?

   (A) to eat   (B) eating   (C) to eating   (D) to be eaten

4. Don't hesitate _____ me when you come to Japan.

   (A) contacting   (B) to be contacting   (C) to contact   (D) in contacting

5. Tom can't afford _____ such an expensive car.

   (A) buying   (B) to buying   (C) to buy   (D) to be bought

▌ Dialogue

対話文を聞いた後、ペアで ☐ の部分を入れ替えて練習しましょう. 最後は、☐ の部分を自分で考えて対話練習しましょう. 🎧 2-40

Ken and Mary are talking about karuta.

Ken: Do you know how to | play *karuta* |? ¹

Mary: No, I don't. It sounds interesting, though. I | like playing games |. ²

Ken: OK, I'll come to your place tomorrow and teach you.

Mary: Great, | I'm looking forward to trying it |. ³

	1	2	3
対話 ①	do origami	enjoy making things	I'm interested in having a go
対話 ②	make sushi	love cooking	I can't wait to eat it
対話 ③	write haiku	am interested in Japanese culture	I'm really excited

*to have a go（やってみる）

Let's check some more!

● 目的語に動名詞しかとらない動詞、不定詞しかとらない動詞、両方とるが意味が異なる動詞があります。

● 動名詞と現在分詞の形は同じですが、用法が違います。

Reading : *Let's Learn Old Japanese Sayings by Playing Karuta.*

英文を読んで質問に答えましょう。 2-41

efuda (torifuda)   *yomifuda*

You get old to obey your son.

Have you ever played the Japanese card game *karuta*? *Karuta* is based on old Japanese sayings. Many sayings date from more than 200 years ago. In order to play *karuta*, you need (① to prepare / preparing) two sets of 48 cards. You find pictures on one half of the cards with a different *hiragana* (Japanese syllable). This set is called *efuda* or *torifuda*. You will find Japanese sayings on the other half of the set called *yomifuda*. Each saying starts with a different *hiragana* and all the different *hiragana* are used only once. In a game, one person reads aloud each *yomifuda* and players attempt (② to grab / grabbing) the correct *efuda*. You win by (③ to get / getting) the most *efuda* cards. Playing *karuta* has always been a popular family game. Adults expect their children (④ to learn / learning) the written language by playing *karuta*.

....

to date from 〜にさかのぼる   **to grab** つかむ

A. 文中の (   ) の中から適語を選びましょう。

B. 1〜5の質問文を読んで英語で答えましょう。

1. How many sets of cards do you need to play *karuta*?

_____

2. How many cards are there in one set?

_____

3. What do you have to do if you want to win?

_____

4. What do adults expect children to do by playing *karuta*?

_____

5. How old are many of the sayings on the cards?

_____

▮ Writing

A. 英文を読んで問いに答えましょう。　(CD) 2-42

> My grandmother is 70 years old. She worked hard at home all her life, but now she has retired. She has recently become a university student. She didn't have a chance to study when she was young, so she decided to join her local university as a mature student. She says that studying is hard, but learning is a lot of fun. She says, "_____"

Q. What does she say? Choose one of the old sayings from the box below.

_____

```
· Seeing is believing.              · Actions speak louder than words.
· A friend in need is a friend indeed.  · It is no use crying over spilt milk.
· You are never too old to learn.     · It is easy to propose impossible
· All is well that ends well.            remedies.
```

B. 上記のold sayingsの一つ、あるいは、自分の好きなold sayingを使って、自分の経験したことを書いてみましょう。

_____

_____

_____

_____

_____

_____

_____

Professions 関係詞

世の中には、どのような職業があるのでしょうか？このユニットでは、様々な職業を通して、人、事物、場所を説明するのに便利な関係詞の使い方を学びましょう。

■ Vocabulary　英語の意味を下の日本語から選びましょう。 🔊 2-43

1. magnifying glass (　　)　　2. interpreter (　　)　　3. laboratory (　　)
4. priest (　　)　　　　　　　5. conference (　　)　　6. bargain (　　)
7. to take care of (　　)　　8. to create (　　)　　　9. to experiment (　　)
10. to contribute (　　)

a. 会議	b. 通訳	c. 貢献する	d. 実験する	e. 実験室
f. 世話をする	g. 作る	h. 特価品	i. 拡大鏡	j. 司祭

■ Warm-up : Various Jobs

絵と関連する職業名、物、場所を下のボックスから選んで、空欄にアルファベットを書きましょう。

a. church	b. gardener	c. gun	d. interpreter
e. laboratory	f. magnifying glass		

	①	②	③	④	⑤	⑥
職業名	scientist	detective	priest		policeman	
もの	test tubes		the Bible	ladder		dictionary
場所		Baker Street		garden	police station	conference

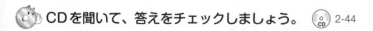 CDを聞いて、答えをチェックしましょう。 🔊 2-44

もう一度CDを聞き、下の（　）を埋めて、答えを確認しましょう。　**repeat**　2-44

1. This is a place (　　　　　　　) a scientist does experiments. He/She sometimes uses test tubes there.

2. This is a thing (　　　　　　) you look through to enlarge objects. Sherlock Holmes, (　　　　　　) lives on Baker Street, is a detective (　　　　　) often uses one.

3. This is a place (　　　　　　　) you go to pray. You sometimes meet priests there. They often read the Bible there. It is a very peaceful place.

4. This is a person (　　　　　　　) works in a garden, uses a rake,* and takes care of plants.

5. This is a thing (　　　　　　) a police officer uses to protect people. He/She works at a police station and usually carries one on his/her belt.

6. This is a person (　　　　　　　) speaks at least two languages. This person helps people from different countries communicate with each other. A dictionary is a useful thing (　　　　　　) he/she needs when working at a conference.

·····················
*4. **rake** 熊手

▨ Grammar Point：関係詞（who, which, where）

▶関係詞は二つの文章を関係づけて結びつける働きをします。主なものに下のような関係代名詞と関係副詞があります。

先行詞	関係代名詞	節の中の働き	例文
人	who/that	主格	An inventor is **a person** <u>who creates new things</u>. 新しいものを作り出す人
	whose	所有格	An inventor is **a person** <u>whose job is to invent new things</u>. 仕事が新しいものを発明する人
	whom/that	目的格	An inventor is **a person** <u>whom many people respect</u>. 多くの人々が尊敬する人

先行詞	関係代名詞	節の中の働き	例 文
事物	which / that	主格	An elephant is **an animal** <u>which lives in a tropical area</u>. 熱帯にすむ動物
	whose / ～of which	所有格	An elephant is **an animal** <u>whose trunk is very long</u>. 鼻がとても長い動物
	which / that	目的格	A zoo is **a place** <u>which many people visit</u>. 多くの人々が訪れる場所

＊アメリカ英語では、which よりも that のほうがより一般的です。
＊動物が先行詞の場合、擬人化して who を使用する場合もあります。

先行詞	関係副詞	節の中の働き	例 文
場所	where / that	副詞	A zoo is **a place** <u>where many animals live</u>. 多くの動物がすむ場所

▌Grammar Practice

A. (　　) 内の語を並べ替えて、意味の通る英文にしましょう.

1. This is the computer (bought, the, I , which, day) before yesterday.
   It was a real bargain.

   _____

2. The girl (Tom, whom, the, met, at) party goes to college. She is very intelligent.

   _____

3. Tom, (father, speaks, whose, Japanese, fluent), is from America. He can't
   speak Japanese at all.

   _____

4. Carol is a bookworm. A bookworm is a (enjoys, a, who, person, reading) lot
   of books.

   _____

5. Jim is a millionaire. He lives in a house (a, which, swimming, has, pool).

   _____

B. 選択肢の中で最も適切なものを選び、1〜5の英文を完成させましょう。

1. This is the school _____ I attended.
   (A) which   (B) who   (C) where   (D) whose

2. I met a person _____ everybody knows from television.
   (A) which   (B) who   (C) whom   (D) whose

3. Tom has a pet dog _____ takes care of a kitten.
   (A) that   (B) where   (C) whom   (D) whose

4. Are you the girl _____ brother I know?
   (A) who   (B) whom   (C) whose   (D) which

5. Windsor Castle is the place _____ Queen Elizabeth lives.
   (A) which   (B) whose   (C) where   (D) what

▌ Dialogue

対話文を聞いた後、ペアで ☐ の部分を入れ替えて練習しましょう。 最後は、☐ の部分を自分で考えて対話練習しましょう。 🎧 2-45

Kay and Jonathan are talking about a party.

Kay: I'm having a party next Saturday. Would you like to come?

Jonathan: Sounds good. Would you like me to bring something?

Kay: Yes, could you bring . . . oh, what's the word . . . something that you | use to open bottles |?[1]

Jonathan: | A corkscrew |?[2]

Kay: Yes, that's right.

	1. 持参する物の説明	2. 持参する物
対話 ①	use to keep drinks cool	an icebox
対話 ②	usually serve at parties	some snacks
対話 ③	often eat at a movie theater	popcorn

Let's check some more!

- 関係代名詞 that のみを使用する場合があるので注意しましょう。
- 関係副詞には where 以外に when, why, how などがあります。

Reading : *Edison, the Greatest Inventor* 2-46

An inventor is a person who creates new things. Edison, who lived from 1847 to 1931, was one of the greatest inventors in the world. In his childhood, he was not considered to be clever. His schooling lasted only for three months. Then he stayed home, where his mother taught him to read and how to experiment. Later in his life, Edison created the phonograph, which was an old-fashioned record player. He also invented the incandescent lamp, which made light by using electricy. He also made the motion-picture projector, which contributed a great deal to people's education and entertainment. Today you can find his inventions everywhere. Because of his inventions, you live in a world where you can watch a movie or listen to music and where you can even read at night.

....

phonograph 蓄音機　**incandescent lamp** 白熱灯
motion-picture projector 映写機

A. 文中の関係詞に下線を引いて、先行詞に○をつけましょう。

B. 質問文を読んで英語で答えましょう。

1. What does an inventor do?

   _____

2. Was Edison educated at school?

   _____

3. What was the phonograph?

   _____

4. How does the incandescent lamp make light?

   _____

5. Where can you find Edison's inventions at present?

   _____

■ Writing

A. 適当な名詞（職業名、物、場所）を下記のリストから選び空欄を埋めて、英文を完成させましょう。

architect, bank, Bible, chalk, dentist, hospital, laboratory, lawyer, marathon runner, mathematician, millionaire, mountain climber, painter, police station, teacher

1. An (   ) is a person who <u>designs houses</u>.
2. A (   ) is a person who <u>paints</u>.
3. A (   ) is a place where <u>a scientist does experiments</u>.
4. A (   ) is a place where <u>doctors help people with health problems</u>.
5. A (   ) is a person who <u>stands up for people's rights</u>.
6. A (   ) is a place where <u>police officers work to protect people</u>.
7. A (   ) is a person who <u>helps people learn</u>.
8. A (   ) is a person who <u>finds correct solutions for problems</u>.
9. A (   ) is a place where <u>you can keep your wealth safe</u>.
10. A (   ) is a person who <u>has a lot of stamina</u>.
11. A (   ) is a person who <u>makes his way to the top of a mountain</u>.
12. A (   ) is a person who <u>is extremely rich</u>.
13. A piece of (   ) is a thing which <u>teachers use</u>.
14. A (   ) is a person who <u>takes care of your teeth</u>.
15. The (   ) is a book which <u>priests use.</u>

B. 使いたい関係詞を選び○をして、文章を完成させましょう.

1. I would like to marry a person (who / whose / whom)_____.
2. I would like to be a person (who / whose / whom)_____.
3. I would like to live in the neighborhood (which / where)_____.
4. I would like to buy a thing (which / whose)_____.
5. I would like to live in a house (which / where)_____.
6. I would like to have a friend (who / whose / whom)_____.
7. I would like to eat something (which / whose)_____.
8. I would like to travel to a place (which / where)_____.
9. I would like to keep a pet (which / whose)_____.
10. I would like to have a job (which / whose)_____.

What If 仮定法

日常会話の中で、現実離れした話題はよくでてきます。このユニットでは、現実にはありえない、起こりそうもないことを、仮定法を使って表現する方法を学びましょう。

■ Vocabulary 英語の意味を下の日本語から選びましょう。 (CD) 2-47

1. invisible ( )   2. to describe ( )   3. to break down ( )
4. to accept ( )   5. to throw a party ( )   6. immediately ( )
7. to suffer ( )   8. mansion ( )   9. disease ( )   10. to give up ( )

a. あきらめる	b. 受け入れる	c. 故障する	d. すぐに	e. 説明する
f. 病気	g. パーティを催す	h. 大邸宅	i. 目に見えない	j. 苦しむ／病む

■ Warm-up : Interviews

下の1～6はインタビューの質問です。これに対する答えの中に含まれそうな語句をa)～f)から選んで線で結びましょう。

1. What would you do if you were invisible for a day?	a) a cheetah
2. What would you do if you were a teacher and your students didn't do their homework?	b) say thank you anyway
3. What animal would you choose if you had to describe yourself as an animal?	c) live in the Edo period
4. What would you do if you went driving and the car suddenly broke down?	d) go to a musical without a ticket
5. What would you do if your best friend gave you a present you didn't like?	e) make them stay after school
6. Which period would you go to if you could go back to the past?	f) call for help

 CDを聞いて、答えをチェックしましょう。 2-48

もう一度CDを聞き、下の (　) を埋めて、答えを確認しましょう。　**repeat** 🔘CD 2-48

1. If I (　　　　　) invisible, I (　　　　　) (　　　　　) to see a musical without buying a ticket.

2. If I (　　　　　) a teacher and my students (　　　　　) (　　　　　) their homework, I (　　　　　) (　　　　　) them stay after school.

3. If I (　　　　　) to describe myself as an animal, I (　　　　　) (　　　　　) a cheetah.

4. If I (　　　　　) (　　　　　) and the car suddenly (　　　　　) down, I (　　　　　) (　　　　　) my friend for help.

5. If my best friend (　　　　　) me a present I (　　　　　) (　　　　　), I (　　　　　) (　　　　　) thank you anyway.

6. If I (　　　　　) (　　　　　) back to the past, I (　　　　　) (　　　　　) to the Edo period. I (　　　　　) I (　　　　　) (　　　　　) a good friend of Tokugawa Ieyasu.

▮ **Grammar Point**：仮定法（仮定法過去）
<If＋主＋動詞の過去形, 主＋would＋動詞の原形＞で「もし〜なら、…だろうに」を表す

▶仮定法過去（現実にはありえない、起こりそうもない仮定の話）

If＋主語＋動詞の過去形、主語＋should, would, could, might＋動詞の原形
もし〜なら…だろう
If I were you, I would follow his advice. 私があなたの立場なら、彼の忠告に従います。（私は絶対にあなたにはなりえない）

▶願望表現（現在実現不可能な願い）

I wish / If only　主語＋(助)動詞の過去形
〜ならよいのになぁ
I wish I were a bird. 鳥だったらいいのになぁ。（人間は絶対に鳥にはなりえない。）
If only I could speak English like a native speaker. ネイティブのように英語がしゃべれたらなぁ。（漠然と思っているだけでは、実現不可能。）

■ Grammar Practice

A. 間違いを訂正して、全文を書き直しましょう。

1. If he were ten years younger, he will be able to run faster.

   _____

2. If I am you, I would not drive in the snow.

   _____

3. If animals could talk, we learn a lot about the animal world.

   _____

4. If Mary knew about Bill's past, she will not marry him.

   _____

5. I wish my friend are here to help me.

   _____

B. 選択肢の中で最も適切なものを選び、1〜5の英文を完成させましょう.

1. If I were the richest person in the world, I _____ an island.
   (A) will buy   (B) buy   (C) would buy   (D) bought

2. I wish I _____ a rich.
   (A) am   (B) is   (C) were   (D) can be

3. What would you do if your friend _____ a lot of money from you and never returned it to you?
   (A) borrows   (B) will borrow   (C) is borrowed   (D) borrowed

4. If I were you, I _____ to hospital immediately.
   (A) go   (B) will go   (C) would go   (D) went

5. If there _____ no television in the world, people would read more.
   (A) is   (B) will be   (C) could be   (D) were

■ Dialogue

CDを聞いて対話文の（　　）を埋めましょう。ペアで対話練習をしましょう。　(CD) 2-49

Emily and David are talking about their impossible dreams.

Emily: What (　　　　　) you (　　　　　　) if you (　　　　　　) 300 million
yen in the lottery?

David: I (　　　　) (　　　　　　) an island near Hawaii.

Emily: And what (　　　　　) you (　　　　　) there?

David: I (　　　　) (　　　　　　) a mansion there and throw a big party
every day.

Emily: (　　　　　) you (　　　　　　) me to the parties?

David: Of course.

Reading : *Tuesdays with Morrie* 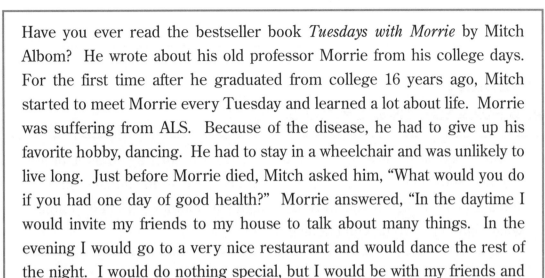 2-50

Have you ever read the bestseller book *Tuesdays with Morrie* by Mitch Albom? He wrote about his old professor Morrie from his college days. For the first time after he graduated from college 16 years ago, Mitch started to meet Morrie every Tuesday and learned a lot about life. Morrie was suffering from ALS. Because of the disease, he had to give up his favorite hobby, dancing. He had to stay in a wheelchair and was unlikely to live long. Just before Morrie died, Mitch asked him, "What would you do if you had one day of good health?" Morrie answered, "In the daytime I would invite my friends to my house to talk about many things. In the evening I would go to a very nice restaurant and would dance the rest of the night. I would do nothing special, but I would be with my friends and family." What would you do if you were Morrie?

....

ALS = amyotrophic lateral sclerosis = Lou Gehrig's disease = 筋萎縮性側索硬化症 (急速に筋肉が萎縮し、筋力が低下する難病。発症後3〜5年で死に至る。今のところ治療法は確立されていない。) **wheelchair** 車椅子 **be unlikely to**＋動詞の原形 〜しそうもない

A. 文中の仮定法の部分に下線を引きましょう。

B. 1〜5の質問文を読んで英語で答えましょう。

1. Who wrote *Tuesdays with Morrie*?

_____

2. Who was Morrie?

_____

3. What was Morrie's job?

_____

4. What did Morrie do every Tuesday?

_____

5. If you were very sick and dying and you could live only one day totally in good health, what would you do?

_____

▊ Writing

A. 以下の英文を読んで質問に答えましょう。 🔘2-51

Many people believe that after we die, we are born again as another person. Some people think that you would be born as an animal or insect. What do you think? If you were born again as another person or animal, what kind of life would you choose?

1. Where would you like to be born?

_____

2. When would you like to be born?

_____

3. Would you like to be born as a man, a woman, an animal or an insect?

_____

4. What would you like to do or be?

_____

B. 上記の質問文を参考にして「もし生まれ変わるとしたら〜」というタイトルで英文を書きましょう。

If I were born again,
_____

_____

_____

_____

_____

TEXT PRODUCTION STAFF

edited by
Hiroko Nakazawa

編集
中澤 ひろ子

English-language editing by
Bill Benfield

英文校閲
ビル・ベンフィールド

cover design by
Nobuyoshi Fujino

表紙デザイン
藤野 伸芳

text design by
Miyuki Inde

本文デザイン
印出 美由紀

CD PRODUCTION STAFF

recorded by
Edith Kayumi（AmE）
Jack Merluzzi（AmE）
Karen Hedrick（AmE）

吹き込み者
イーディス・カユミ（アメリカ英語）
ジャック・マルージー（アメリカ英語）
カレン・ヘドリック（アメリカ英語）

Living Grammar ―New Edition―
コミュニケーションのためのベーシック・グラマー ―最新版―

2021年1月25日　初版発行
2024年2月10日　第5刷発行

著　者　山本 厚子・大須賀 直子・真野 千佳子・
　　　　岡本 京子・Benedict Rowlett

発行者　佐野 英一郎

発行所　株式会社 成美堂
　　　　〒101-0052　東京都千代田区神田小川町3-22
　　　　TEL 03-3291-2261　FAX 03-3293-5490
　　　　https://www.seibido.co.jp

印刷・製本　三美印刷(株)

ISBN 978-4-7919-7227-2　　　　　　　　　Printed in Japan